LIVING IN SILENCE

FINDING MY VOICE

CLAIMING MY FREEDOM

PRAISE FOR
LIVING IN SILENCE

"We congratulate Cindy on the courage it took in breaking her silence. The bravery of those willing to come forward and tell of their sexual abuse should be equally matched by our commitment as a culture to hold those abusers accountable."

ALAN AND MARILYN BERGMAN
ACADEMY AWARD WINNING LYRICISTS

"In Living in Silence, Cindy voices the importance and urgency of seeking help, standing strong in your truth, and setting yourself free despite the occurrences and circumstances of your life."

MARIO & FRANNY ARRIZON
BUSINESS MOGULS AND MOTIVATIONAL SPEAKERS

"Living in Silence is a deeply moving and powerful story. Cindy Arevalo writes with sincerity and bravery to testify that there is always hope when you trust in Jesus Christ, especially when hope seems out of reach."

PHIL LIBERATORE, CPA

Copyright © 2021 by Cindy Arevalo

All rights reserved. No part of this publication may be reproduced, distributed, or transmitted in any form or by any means, including photocopying, recording, or other electronic or mechanical methods, without the prior written permission of the publisher, except in the case of brief quotations embodied in critical reviews and certain other noncommercial uses permitted by copyright law. For permission requests, write to the publisher at the address below.

Fedd Books
P.O. Box 341973
Austin, TX 78734
www.thefeddagency.com
Published in association with The Fedd Agency, Inc., a literary agency.

ISBN: 978-1-949784-68-8
eISBN: 978-1-949784-69-5

Library of Congress Control Number: 2021906571

Printed in the United States of America

Cover Image: Juan Perez
Cover Design: Deryn Pieterse

First Edition 15 14 13 12 11 / 10 9 8 7 6 5 4 3 2

TO THE SURVIVORS . . .

CONTENTS

PROLOGUE ix
  1 COFFEE GIRL 1
  2 BOILING A FROG 15
  3 DAMAGED GOODS..31
  4 THE STALKER 47
  5 RECONNECTED...71
  6 INDEBTED 93
  7 UNEXPECTED TWIST 111
  8 SPEAKING UP 125
  9 THE STAKEOUT 137
  10 SEVERING TIES 153
EPILOGUE 165
ADDITIONAL RESOURCES 169
HELPFUL BIBLE VERSES 171
ACKNOWLEDGMENTS 175

PROLOGUE

I don't really know how to start telling my story. I mean, obviously I can give you a chronological series of events. But telling you my story in a way that you'll hear what I have to say? Telling my story in such a way that you won't write me off as some sort of delinquent, a problem child, or someone who was asking for it? Or, at the very least, telling my story so that you won't write off what happened to me because of my dysfunctional family situation? That's a harder thing to figure out.

When survivors of sexual assault or rape share their stories, especially when the attacks are repeated by the same perpetrator, people often seem unwilling to listen. Our stories of resilience, courage in the face of evil, and taking back control of our lives and bodies are overshadowed by harmful assumptions shaped by pernicious societal biases meant to discredit us or diminish the responsibility of our abuser.

"Well, dressed like that…"

"She was drunk, what did she expect?!"

"She flirted with him."

"Oh, she wanted it."

"Boys can't be overpowered like that."

"Why didn't they just tell someone?"

"How could they not know that was wrong?"

Sound familiar?

I met my abuser when I was fourteen. I don't know what your life was like at fourteen, but at that age, I was basically a jumbled mess of hormones with a rapidly developing body that I didn't understand. Puberty was busy doing its thing, and my body was beginning that awkward evolution from child to young adult. I felt like a silent bystander, watching the shape and size of my body transform before my very eyes without any control over what was happening. During these years, things just didn't seem to fit quite right: my arms were too long, my frame was too thin, and I had acne. *Oh, the acne ...*

    I was also a skinny kid, but I always felt like my arms were extra bony. I grew up in Southern California—a place known for its warm, sunny climate—where shorts and sleeveless tops at any time of year are the norm. When I attempted to be trendy and wear spaghetti strap shirts, I hated how they drew attention to my arms; I felt exposed, naked. On top of that, I broke my nose as a kid, and as it grew with me, its crookedness seemed more pronounced. My teeth pointed in every direction, and my sister never missed a chance to let me know that no one would want to kiss someone with teeth like mine. I was extremely flat-chested, desperately waiting for the day my breasts would grow. Some girls at school would brag about their breasts "coming in overnight" or "over the weekend," and I couldn't help but hope that something like that would soon happen to me too. I wasn't allowed to wear makeup, so my only hope in hiding the acne running rampant on my forehead was to cover it up with my bangs. And, honestly, using my hair as a distraction was a pretty good tactic since I had absolutely no idea how to tame my frizzy, out-of-control locks. Neither my mom nor my sister was too concerned with hair or makeup, so I had to try to figure out how to style my hair on my own. No matter how much product I slapped on or how tightly I tried to pin my hair back, by the end of the day it returned to its natural frizzy state.

As the youngest in my family, I was incredibly sheltered. Because my parents had to work long hours to make ends meet, they set very strict rules about where I could go and what I could wear—and they also had strong opinions about boys. My mom, who herself had a troubled upbringing, set her sights on me marrying someone who could offer me (and her) a better life. My father worried about keeping me safe, but he didn't have the emotional tools to explain that to me, so he did the only thing he knew to do: he imposed on me incredibly strict rules. So, while some of the other kids at school were starting to talk about boyfriends and girlfriends and how "far" they got with their partner, I was still waiting on my first serious boyfriend and my first kiss. My sheltered upbringing meant I was pretty ignorant when it came to relationships, sex, and most means of physical affection. While I felt like I was behind the romantic curve compared to the other kids at my school, and I was certain boys weren't remotely interested in me, I know now that my middle school romance experience was pretty standard. Despite being a couple years from driving and a few more years from being a legal adult, I was still very much a kid.

I was a pretty typical eager-to-please, obedient kid who didn't have any reason to second guess an adult's intentions, particularly one in a position of authority—one I was told I was supposed to listen to and trust. And that's exactly what happened. Kip Arnold was a substitute teacher for my P.E. class who asked me to hold his coffee and help him out during class. But what started as a pretty normal day soon turned into a nightmare worse than I could have ever imagined. What follows is the story of how he used his role as a teacher to gain my trust, used my school's lack of accountability to get unfettered access to me during the school day, and ultimately used my childhood innocence against me just before he stole it. He groomed me so that he was able to repeatedly rape me, assault me, threaten me, stalk me, and blackmail me.

For years he had me convinced that his abuse was normal, and when I began to fight back, he convinced me that I was the problem. He convinced me it was better to stay quiet. He convinced me that I was worthless—that I was doing something that made me *deserving* of his abuse.

And that's why I want to be sure I start this story off on the right foot. The way he was able to manipulate me and bend the truth to fit his narrative, and the way he was able to convince me that I did something to deserve the things he did to me, kept me silent for years. Those same manipulation and fear tactics keep scores of other victims of sexual assault and rape silent. Because, whether it is our abuser telling us we are guilty or society perceiving us this way, we are convinced that we somehow deserved what happened to us.

Unfortunately, our society has perpetuated the idea that survivors of rape did something—or neglected to do something—to merit their attack. Maybe they were careless, too drunk, dressed too provocatively, or a litany of other excuses that pile the burden of guilt onto the victim until it stifles them to silence—even if they were a child when it happened. Maybe we've developed that societal prejudice as a defense mechanism because we don't want to believe the regular people around us who we see in school, at church, or at the store—as opposed to hardened, violent criminals who only hide in the shadows and "bad parts of town"—are capable of rape. Maybe we react to survivors that way because it is too easy to see ourselves, or our children, in the survivor's shoes, and we don't want to think anything like that can ever happen so close to home.

Whatever our reasons for being skeptical of stories of rape or overly critical of survivors and their stories, I invite you to step away from those prejudices for a moment. Throughout this book, I invite you to walk alongside me as I tell you about how a teacher groomed me, manipulated me, gaslit me, and subjected me to years of fear, abuse, and rape. As I tell you my story, I want you to meet that awkward fourteen-year-old girl who felt like she wasn't in control of her own body, was confused by her thoughts, and was ashamed and embarrassed about how she looked—the girl who ultimately just wanted to find a place where she was accepted, loved, and heard. I want you to see her go from a shy girl too scared to rock the boat—who was told time and again that her instincts and feelings were wrong and that her voice was too much—to a woman who boldly spoke her truth, even when it scared her. Whether you are a survivor yourself or an acquaintance of one; whether you are a parent, teacher, government official, church leader, or anyone who works closely with young people; whether you are male or female—I want you to walk that journey with me so that in hearing my story and how I found my voice, you see that you can find yours too.

CHAPTER ONE
COFFEE GIRL

I wasn't used to being seen. Deep down I knew my parents loved me, but for various reasons they didn't have as much time for me as I would have liked. Both my mother and my father immigrated to the United States from El Salvador as adults, though they didn't meet until they were in America. My dad never talked much about his life in El Salvador, except to say that although he had a home, he chose to spend most of his time hanging out and even sleeping on the streets with other children. Reading between the lines, I understood that my dad must have had a difficult upbringing, and he had come to the U.S. to try to forge a better life.

My mother, on the other hand, was never shy about sharing her experiences in El Salvador. To put it plainly, her life was filled with injustices and tragedy. She grew up poor and lived in a hastily constructed hut with an aluminum roof. Her father wasn't around, and her mother passed away when she was very young, so she was raised by her grandmother. When my great-grandmother passed, my mom had no one to care for her and was moved to a state-run boarding school. It was a harsh environment, and my mom became pregnant with my older sister when she was a teenager; she was trapped in an abusive relationship with my sister's father. She had one other child in El Salvador, a boy, but he died before he was even a year old.

She came to America in her thirties, leaving my sister behind with family so she could build a life in the States. When she met my dad, they were adults with a lot of life and a lot of pain behind them. They had come to a new country on their own, where neither of them spoke the language, and forged their own paths. When they got married, their attitude toward family wasn't really about linking arms and facing the world together; it was more about taking care of themselves first and building something that would keep them secure because no one else would look out for them. My parents lived in separate rooms, split bills, and essentially lived separate lives. This was the family dynamic I was born into, and not long after that, my mother brought my sister from El Salvador to live with us. A strong sense of self-preservation was passed on to me, and for a long time, I didn't think anything was amiss with how my family functioned. It wasn't until much later, when I met the man who would become my husband and observed the love and loyalty in his family, that I began to understand how dysfunctional my family was.

But at fourteen, I didn't realize anything was out of the ordinary about my upbringing. For me, isolation was just a reality. I spent most of my time in my room, whether I was eating dinner, doing homework, or just relaxing on a weekend. We even spent holidays apart. On Thanksgiving, my mom would cook a big dinner and set it out in the kitchen, and we all went in, built up a plate, and headed off to our rooms to eat alone.

My parents worked constantly, with my mom spending the day cleaning houses and my dad working nights as a security guard. My older sister still lived with us, along with her husband and child, but she was several years my senior and very busy with her own job and family. Understandably, everyone seemed to be tired a lot. So they didn't have a lot of space in their lives to deal with an overemotional teenager. If I went to them with a concern, a homework issue, or a question, I was often met with a sigh and the suggestion to handle it myself because they had been working all day and were tired. It wasn't long before I got the message: I was too demanding and exhausting. My parents and older sister worked so hard; the least I could do was keep quiet, keep the peace at home, and not cause any trouble. The way my homelife worked was that each person looked out for themselves first, and if everyone did their part and stayed in their lane, everything would be okay.

But my parents still kept tabs on me, and one of the ways they did this was by enforcing strict rules. My father was a cultural Catholic, but my mother had converted to Christianity and always pressured me to go to church and be a Christian. She even pressured me to get baptized, which I didn't understand since I had been baptized as a baby. Regardless, I wasn't remotely interested in Christianity or faith, and I definitely wasn't looking to change my life or my habits. I'm sure there was also a bit of extra protection surrounding me because I was the baby of the family. Maybe my parents thought that because they worked so much, they had to make strict rules to keep me in line when they weren't around. Whatever the reason, I was barred from wearing makeup and dating, and my parents were very strict about how late I stayed out and who I spent time with. Any attempt to test those boundaries was met with swift consequences.

For example, I once curled my eyelashes, and my sister thought I had put on mascara. She immediately dragged me to my mother, who gave me a smack and an intense verbal beat-down, shaming me for supposedly breaking the rules and questioning my morals for deciding to wear makeup at such a young age. When I tried to explain that I hadn't been putting on makeup, I only angered her further, so I quickly found out it was better to stay quiet. Taking the punishment was easier, even if it was undeserved. Another time, I decided to wear a spaghetti strap shirt. My dad and aunt saw me and immediately lashed out at me. All at once, I heard things like:

"What are you wearing?! You look naked!"

"How could you wear that! You're disgusting!"

"What were you thinking?"

"Put some clothes on!"

I was only eleven. What I thought was a totally innocent wardrobe choice (we did, after all, live in a mild climate) would forever be etched in my mind as the source of much humiliation and embarrassment. From that point on, their words constantly echoed in my head if I wore anything remotely revealing. Because of their words and my own extreme self-consciousness about my body, I tended to cover up and dress extra modestly. And when I say "cover up," I mean it. Even in the middle of the hot California summer, I usually wore long-sleeved sweaters or a puffy Dodger's jacket. I was sweaty, but I felt more comfortable hiding my body. I didn't want to risk feeling exposed or disgusting.

Even though I dressed modestly, I still couldn't escape the criticism about my body. My mom and sister would make jokes about my small chest, calling my breasts "mosquito bites." After I broke my nose, my mom would constantly bemoan how unsightly it looked, and my sister would tell me my crooked teeth would stop anyone from ever wanting to kiss me. Comments about my body were almost always negative and left me feeling worthless and ashamed. I tried my best to do what I was told and make my family happy because I so often felt like I was failing at things that were far beyond my control.

That quiet nature and sheltered family life also meant I was pretty naïve. As I entered my teen years, my friends at school were starting to talk more about boyfriends and girlfriends, and we heard stories about couples in the school who had sexual or romantic experiences. Much of the talk was probably exaggerated or even made up, but it still made me feel like I was falling behind—I hadn't even kissed a boy. I believed my body was disgusting, disfigured, and messed up beyond my control: I wasn't getting boobs like the other girls around me, didn't have a boyfriend, and wasn't even sure what I was supposed to do with a boy even if we did go out.

And then I met Kip Arnold. From that very first day, he called me "Coffee Girl"; he paid attention to me. At the beginning of my eighth-grade year in 2004, he substituted for my P.E. class, and like most subs, he needed a bit of help. So he asked me to do small things throughout the period like hold his coffee, answer questions, and put away the equipment. I didn't think much of it and went on with my day.

Soon after, he was hired in a permanent capacity at my school, so I frequently saw him in the halls, when I was in my own P.E. class, or if he subbed for one of my classes. Whenever he saw me, he got a big smile on his face, waved, and said, "Hey! It's Coffee Girl!"

As a kid who was relatively shy, I usually wasn't the one picked out of a crowd like this, so I couldn't help but feel a little excited by the attention. Mr. Arnold was the cool new teacher. He let us get away with more stuff in class, and he liked to talk about movies and crack jokes. He also had a large frame and was one of the few white people on my school's multi-cultural campus, so he physically stood out. And for some reason, I seemed to be one of his favorites.

I'd been noticed before, of course, like when my dad and my aunt commented on my spaghetti strap shirt. But that's not what was happening with Arnold. I felt like he saw me in a different way—that he saw something special in me. He didn't just call me "Coffee Girl." He inquired about my day and genuinely seem interested in the answer. Our P.E. classes were mostly held outdoors, and several classes would share the same area, so even if I wasn't in his class, I was near him. He often approached my

P.E. teacher, Mr. Valdemar, to get me out of my P.E. class and into his, or he sent me to ask Mr. Valdemar myself. At times, Mr. Valdemar seemed hesitant to allow me to move to Arnold's class, but he didn't say anything and never reported it.

I didn't think anything was strange about changing teachers. After all, I was just helping him out during my P.E. class, and it wasn't like I was missing some important notes or anything. It was gym, and wasn't in helpful to build a good rapport with a teacher? College and job applications always asked for references, and I wanted to please my parents by choosing a profession they'd be proud of, like nursing or teaching, so I knew it would be good to have a teacher who could talk me up in my future endeavors.

Besides, Mr. Arnold was nice. He listened to me, and I always felt safe talking to him about my problems. It felt so good to know there was someone out there who truly wanted to take the time to get to know me as a person and believed what I had to say was important. I never felt embarrassed being honest with him. I didn't realize it then, but he was starting to fill a fatherly role that I so desperately needed in my life. Finally, I had an adult who cared about me, wanted to hear my heart, and was willing to take the time to teach and explain things to me. Of course, at age fourteen, I didn't realize what a profound role he was filling for me—how, unlike my own father, he had the time to sit, talk, and give me advice. It wasn't long before my hormonal teenage self turned those feelings of safety into a crush. I didn't think anything would come from the crush, of course; I just really liked spending time with him.

Over time, Mr. Valdemar became increasingly unhappy with Arnold's constant requests for me to be in his class. Finally, he decided to approach me about it and said, "Sunshine, I don't like you hanging around with Mr. Arnold so much." I was taken aback. No one had ever called me "Sunshine," let alone a teacher. But looking in his eyes, I could tell he was genuinely concerned for me. However, before I got the chance to ask him to elaborate, the bell rang. He sent me on my way to class and never brought it up again. I found out later that he also never told the school administration.

I wasn't sure what to think about Mr. Valdemar's warning. Because he never followed up with an explanation, I figured it had to do with him not liking how much of his class I spent elsewhere. I started to get so comfortable spending P.E. with Arnold's class that I sometimes just up and left Mr. Valdemar's class to head over to Arnold's. I figured that had to be why Mr. Valdemar was frustrated, and I didn't really think much of it beyond that.

A few months later, someone else expressed concerns about Kip Arnold. I was casual acquaintances with two other female students whom I saw with Arnold around the school. One day, as we were in the middle of random small talk, one of the girls started looking suspiciously over her shoulder, leaned in, and whispered, "I think Mr. Arnold is really creepy." I frowned and looked at her, unsure of what she meant. But before I could ask what, Arnold himself interrupted us. The girls walked away, and Arnold demanded to know what we were talking about.

"Oh, we were just talking. She said she thought you were kinda creepy." I laughed.

His face grew stern. "What did she mean by that?"

I shrugged. "I don't know. She just said you were kinda creepy. It's not a big deal."

But it was clearly a big deal to him. He didn't like word spreading that he was "creepy." I assumed it was because he didn't like to hear students talking negatively about him. In both the case with my friend and Mr. Valdemar, the conversation had stopped abruptly, and neither of them ever mentioned it again. Even though it was weird for two people to say something, I figured it couldn't be that big of a deal since they only mentioned it once.

While I was only an eighth grader, Arnold began to increase how much time he spent with me. At some point, things began to shift from me helping him outside, with all of the other students around, to him asking me to meet him in a storage closet or office to help him with a task. I also started assisting him outside of class with grading and other administrative tasks. No other teachers had lavished me with such attention, and I believed I had been specially chosen. Plus, Arnold was always so good about asking me about my life. He didn't just ask me about my day or the latest school drama—he asked pointed questions to get to know me and the details of my life.

"What do you want to be when you grow up?"

"Who drives you to and from school?"

"Do you want to have kids?"

"When do you get picked up from school?"

"If you could travel anywhere in the world, where would it be?"

"When do your parents work?"

"What's your most embarrassing moment?"

"How often are you alone at home?"

"What's your biggest dream for your life?"

"Do you live close to family?"

"What's your favorite holiday?"

"Do you have big family holiday celebrations, or are you often on your own?"

I loved how much interest he took in me, and he wasn't stingy with compliments either. Whenever I expressed feelings of self-consciousness or talked disparagingly about my looks, he always shut that talk down and told me how pretty I was. I had only known him a couple of months, but I already felt safe enough to confide in him with my troubles at home, like when I got in a fight with my mom about going to church, when my dad told me I wouldn't amount to anything, or when my sister got angry at me for not doing as many chores as she did. He always made me feel better by telling me how pretty and mature I was and giving me candy. I felt like I could really relate to him. Just like me, he was frequently alone. He told me he lived on a boat, just him and his dog, so he knew what it meant to be lonely. At this point, I found myself alone with him often, helping him in his office or helping him get supplies from storage. I started to notice that he always looked for ways to brush past me or touch me or squeeze my thigh.

But it all happened in such a natural, non-threatening way. Never once did he make me feel like I was in danger or that our interactions were some sort of illicit secret. Instead, I felt like everything we were doing was perfectly normal and that he was just taking an interest in me. He told me I was far more mature than other girls my age. Naturally, I loved having an adult validate my feelings, thoughts, and emotions in such a way that they set me apart from the rest of my age group. Finally someone thought I was more than an exhausting disappointment! It felt good to be valued, and I couldn't help but be excited that this teacher I was crushing on said I was pretty.

It was still the first semester of my eighth-grade year when he gave me his phone number. It seemed pretty innocent at first, as he initially gave me his number because he said he was interested in my older sister. They even set a date together, and he ultimately stood her up. He made up a weird excuse as to why he didn't show but capitalized on the fact that I now had his phone number.

"You should call me sometime," he told me. His face quickly grew solemn. "Keep this between us, though. If anyone found out, it could be really bad. I'd get in really big trouble and so would you. You wouldn't want that, would you?"

I smiled and shook my head. Of course I didn't want to get us into trouble! However, when I got home, I didn't end up calling him. I trusted him and enjoyed our talks, but part of me felt a bit weird about calling a teacher after school hours. I figured he was offering to talk to me on the phone if I needed help, so I wasn't totally sure why he made such a big deal about keeping it a secret, but it didn't bother me. I was used to keeping secrets; I was actually really good at it.

You'd think his insistence about keeping the phone number between us would have been a red flag. Now, as an adult, I know that one way you can train a child to spot a potential predator is to tell them adults don't keep big secrets with kids. But at that time, keeping secrets with both kids and adults was perfectly normal for me. It was kind of the unofficial language of my family. My mom confided in me about where she hid a bit of money from my father and said I wasn't allowed to tell him or anyone else where it was. My dad told me when he found my mom's money and swiped a few bucks, swearing me to secrecy. My cousins would come to me with secrets that I couldn't share with anyone else. It truly wasn't out of the ordinary for someone else, let alone a trusted adult like Mr. Arnold, to come to me with a juicy secret. I wouldn't tell.

The more I helped him out around the school, the more my feelings for him seemed to evolve. I genuinely cared about Mr. Arnold, and I looked forward to spending time with him. I loved knowing I could have the worst day in the world, and I could go straight to Mr. Arnold's office and talk it out, leaving with a smile on my face, a lifted spirit, and a renewed sense of hope and self-worth (and probably some candy in my pocket). He ultimately offered me his number again—reminding me not to tell anyone—and I finally called him after school while my parents were at work. We started talking on the phone a lot, nearly every day. The conversations usually began with me getting the chance to share my thoughts and struggles with him, but they gradually became flirtier.

I was over the moon when he told me that he liked me. Looking back on it now, it's incredibly weird to hear an adult use such childish language to explain their feelings, but at fourteen, that was the most romantic thing he could have ever said to me. My heart skipped a beat, and I tried my best to hide my smile as I admitted, "I like you too." He smiled and told me he was flattered. I wasn't sure what us "liking each other" meant in real terms, not that I was thinking that way, but I was happy to know this guy returned my affections. It felt great.

Later that same day, he told me to meet him in the P.E. office. He told me to be sure no one saw me, or we could get in trouble. I didn't want that, so I made extra sure no one else was around when I went to meet him. When I arrived, he was sitting in a chair, watching the door as I entered. He looked at me in a way I had never seen before. His eyes were focused on me, and he began to breathe heavily. There was so much passion in his eyes, but it wasn't a passion that felt exciting or inviting—it felt like he was admiring something he was about to devour completely. My eyes darted around the room and something from deep within my gut screamed at me to run. But because of where Arnold was sitting and the arrangement of the office, I realized getting out quickly without him stopping me would be almost impossible. So I stayed put.

"I want everything from you," he said breathlessly.

I looked around nervously. "What do you mean?" I asked quietly.

He never answered. What was happening? Before he could take a single step toward me, someone walked into the office. And just like that, the look disappeared, the heavy breathing stopped, and he switched back into normal office mode. I was so confused and started feeling uncomfortable, but I wasn't quite sure what I was supposed to do next.

Our phone conversations continued and soon grew into him asking me questions about how experienced I was with boys in a physical sense. At some point, Arnold started referring to himself as my boyfriend. He took it upon himself to let me know what a romantic relationship was like and how people in love would act around one another. To be honest, I never called him my boyfriend, but I was still happy with our friendship. I tried to forget about that uncomfortable moment in his office.

After all, he was nice, he cared about me, and he made me feel happy when we were together. I hadn't even kissed a boy, so the whole situation was entirely foreign to me and a little exciting. I knew he didn't want anyone to know we were talking but that didn't really make me wonder if what we were doing was wrong. He was my teacher, so surely everything was okay. Plus, ever since I could remember, my mother and older sister had joked about me finding a rich older man to marry. At the back of my mind, I thought that maybe this thing with Arnold was just me getting a head start on finding my older "rich" man.

However, it didn't take long for things to start making me uncomfortable. There were moments where he positioned himself to brush past me so that he could covertly touch my breasts or my bottom. And he started talking more frequently about physical ways that couples expressed their love. Explicit discussions about physical expressions of affection even happened outside of our phone conversations, mostly when we were outside in P.E. Something about the crowds and the noise made him feel hidden, I guess, like he could be as graphic as he wanted and no one would notice.

Of course, I had no idea what was happening and usually didn't understand what he was saying or why he shared what he shared with me. But he loved to let me know the days he wasn't wearing underwear under his gym shorts; it seemed like a weird choice and kind of gross, but I didn't dwell on it. One time, when I was standing with him as he watched his class run laps, he looked at me and a sinister snicker passed his lips as he sat down. I asked what was so funny, and he said, "I have a hard on right now." Of course, I had no idea what that meant, and he explained that he was excited. It was weird, and I didn't totally understand, but he made me feel like these were good things for me to know, like I was somehow privileged to be told this stuff. Plus, he had done such a good job of establishing a firm foundation of trust and safety that I didn't question anything.

But our interactions soon became more than conversations on the track where he made throwaway comments about being hard. When we were on the phone, he continued probing for information on how much I was alone, my family's presence in my life, and other specifics of my day-to-day life. But he also pressed for specifics about what I knew about sex. Every time he found something I had no knowledge of (which was most things), I felt embarrassed, but he never seemed to care. In fact, I got the idea that he actually seemed to like that I was naïve.

With parents who were often gone and a much older sister who had a family of her own to worry about, he knew there really wasn't anyone around to educate me about romance, choices I made with my body, and relationships. He took that as an opportunity to teach me everything he thought I needed to know about romance and relationships, knowing I didn't have anyone to ask if I wanted to confirm his information. But I trusted him, so I had no reason to doubt any of the things he told me or to believe there was anything bad about how much attention he paid me. Our conversations continued to escalate in their explicit nature as he began explaining ways a couple could be physically intimate with each other, and he started talking to me about the idea of having phone sex with him. Slowly but surely, I started wondering if I was maybe in a bit over my head.

CHAPTER TWO
BOILING A FROG

In spite of the way our friendship escalated to a level that was sometimes uncomfortable, the explicit conversations, the increased physical contact, and the weird meeting in his office where he told me he wanted everything from me—I wasn't afraid of Kip Arnold. You know the old saying about boiling a frog? That you slowly increase the heat over time, so by the time the frog realizes it's in danger, it's too late? That's the perfect metaphor for the way Arnold groomed, manipulated, and gaslit me into not noticing how inappropriate our interactions had become.

By the end of my eighth-grade year, Arnold was well aware that I didn't have anyone at home to talk to, so he made sure his door was always open. He knew that with my tumultuous family life, I frequently needed a shoulder to cry on, and he was always incredibly loving and supportive. He also knew my parents worked long hours and that their preferred method of teaching me was to shame me away from negative behavior without explaining *why* something was bad. The fact that my parents prohibited me from dating, for instance, was probably because my mom didn't want me to get pregnant as a teenager. But instead of talking to me openly about dating and sex or allowing me to ask questions in a safe and nonjudgmental way, she issued threats about how much trouble I'd be in and how I'd ruin my life if I even thought about going out with a boy. Unless, of course, he was rich.

So, when Arnold talked to me about sex and relationships, he made the environment feel like a judgment-free zone—at least, he did at first. He didn't try to shame me or scare me out of learning or exploring; he welcomed it! He let me ask questions, understood and validated my curiosity when I did, and never made me feel embarrassed for not knowing something. Of course, he also realized that I had been raised to always acquiesce to people in authority and go with the flow, so he capitalized on that as he "taught" me about relationships.

As my main source of sex education, Arnold made sure to carefully curate the information he gave me so that when I went with the flow, I traveled directly where he wanted me. He made sure I understood that sex and showing love through sex were perfectly normal, even between an adult and a child. He assured me that, because of my maturity, I was basically an adult and ready for a more serious relationship—and everything that entailed. He crafted my foundational understanding of sexuality and romance to fit the mold of what he wanted to do to me. So as things slowly became more sexual, though I wasn't sure I totally understood or felt ready for the things he talked about, he made me feel like it was totally natural. He made me believe I should just relax and go with it.

I continued to talk with Arnold on the phone nearly every day. Despite my growing discomfort, he made me feel like he truly cared about my life. He continued to offer me compliments, call himself my boyfriend, and do his best to make me feel pretty and loved. It was nice, and I loved it. But our phone calls were also becoming increasingly explicit. He shared with me about getting an erection, masturbation, and various sexual acts a couple could engage in together. I could tell from the excitement in his voice that he relished every new act about which he could "educate" me.

I didn't completely understand what he was trying to teach me or why he seemed so excited when it came to talking about sex. Even with his constant reassurances that our relationship was normal and natural, it didn't feel "natural" to talk about any of that stuff with him. But I didn't want to risk upsetting him, so I just tried to steer the conversation in a different direction. I couldn't shake the memory of the look in his eyes when we were alone in his office, and it still frightened me. So I wanted to keep whatever that energy was at arm's length. Unfortunately, my efforts didn't work.

One day, he told me he wanted me to meet him by a storage room on campus after school. He looked at me intently and gave me incredibly strict instructions. "Change out of your P.E. uniform, and make sure no one else is around. When you're sure you're alone—no kids, no teachers, no staff, just you—then head to the storage room. If you're sure no one saw you, wait for me there."

I was a little taken aback by his intensity, but I did what he said. Once everyone was gone and I was certain I was alone, I headed for the storage room. As I stood around waiting for him, nervous and apprehensive about what might happen, he finally opened the door. My heart stopped when I saw the look in his eyes. It was the same look he had in his eyes in his office that day along with the heavy breathing, the intensity—all of it. It was like he was a hunter, and I was his prey. The safe, cool, fun teacher had suddenly morphed into a hungry, lust-filled adult who was on the prowl. I didn't try to run away. Even if that thought had crossed my mind, he was much larger than me and I would have been no match. He stepped closer to me and immediately started touching me. He put his hands between my legs, grabbed my butt, pushed his hand up my shirt to feel my breasts, and then leaned down and started kissing me.

That was my first kiss. I was fourteen. He was in his forties.

During the entire encounter, I was paralyzed by panic. I didn't know what to do. Was this wrong? Was this okay? Was this a normal thing to happen? I had no idea! I knew I felt nervous, but I wasn't exactly sure why. Was I scared? Was I nervous because this was new or maybe because I was feeling excited? I knew I was a bit behind the curve when it came to romance, so I wasn't sure if this was just what people my age did. And Arnold was doing things he had explained to me on the phone. In the end, I reasoned that this had to be natural. Right?

Regardless of what he "taught" me, I didn't love the feeling of him kissing and touching me. Instinctively, I wanted to get away from him, and I felt scared and embarrassed to have another person be so intimate with me. But I told myself to keep quiet and not cause trouble. Mr. Arnold certainly wouldn't do anything to hurt me, would he? My heart pounded and my mind raced as I tried to figure out exactly what was happening and how I needed to respond. I wasn't sure what I was supposed to do, but when Arnold finally pulled away from me, I could see the excitement and elation in his eyes. I might have been a big ball of confusion, fear, and nerves but one thing was clear: he thought the entire interaction was amazing. Nothing happened beyond that, and I left the room to head home. He begged me to stay, but I told him my dad was waiting to pick me up and that I couldn't keep him waiting any longer. Eventually, he let me go, and I made my way to my dad as I tried desperately to sort out what had happened.

Later that night, Arnold called me. It was one of the only times after he attacked me that he asked me how I felt. I was still in shock, and the entire situation felt far too intense for me—not to mention the fact that it was my first kiss. But it was clear from his voice that he was still euphoric about what happened. I didn't want to make him feel bad, so I lied and told him that I had enjoyed the encounter just as much as he did. Arnold had done such a good job of manipulating me that I felt that if I even hinted at being anything short of over the moon about our kiss, then I would be the bad guy for hurting his feelings. He took my silence as a green light to go into graphic detail. He explained how touching me made him feel, how I tasted to him, and how aroused he was right then on the phone. And the entire time, I just felt grossed out and incredibly uncomfortable. How could something that made him feel so great make me the complete opposite? Was something wrong with me? He always said I was so mature, so why couldn't I seem to handle this if I was so grown-up?

Time passed, and I finished my final year of middle school. With my freshman year of high school on the horizon, I assumed things with Arnold would fizzle out since we would be in different schools and wouldn't see each other every day. However, we spent more time engaging in phone sex or talking about various sexual things that he wanted to teach me. These conversations were upsetting, but I kept telling myself that my instincts must be wrong—that we cared about one another, so it was okay. And if that didn't work, Arnold was always quick to tell me that things like fingering, oral sex, or anal sex were perfectly normal, beautiful, and fun ways for couples who really loved each other to express their love. And so, in a matter of months, I went from a fourteen-year-old girl who was so sheltered that she felt exposed wearing a tank top in public, to a girl who had not only kissed a grown man but was also touched by one.

Eventually, my older sister found out about my phone conversations with Arnold when she picked up the phone one afternoon while I was talking with him. She didn't hear anything other than us ending the conversation and hanging up, but it was enough to worry her. She charged upstairs to yell at me—her go-to method of correcting me if I stepped out of line. I never considered my sister as someone I could confide in if I had a problem, especially if it included a boy (and even more so if that boy was actually a teacher). When she confronted me, my mind was practically smoking; I was in a panic trying to figure out how to get out of the situation. I knew my phone conversations with Arnold were meant to be a secret, so I had to tread carefully. And my sister was the last person I could trust with such an important secret.

"Who was that on the phone?" she demanded.

"It was no one. Just a boy from school."

"I heard you two on the phone. That was no boy—that was a man's voice. Who were you talking to?"

"Relax! It was just a boy from school! I don't know what you thought you heard, but it's nothing!"

She nodded curtly and rushed off to find my mother. My heart raced as I tried to figure out how to escape this mess. I listened to her telling my mother what she heard on the phone. In seconds, my mom rushed toward me, demanding to know who I'd been talking to. But I was good with secrets, so I kept insisting it was just a boy from school. My sister grabbed the phone and dialed *69 to reverse trace the number from the last phone call. When Arnold answered, thinking it was me, he was met with an incredibly unpleasant surprise as my sister ripped into him.

"Listen! I don't know who this is, but my sister is a *child*! Don't you *ever* think about calling this number again or talking to my sister again or I will call the cops on your ass so fast your *head will spin*!"

She sputtered out a few more profanity-laced threats and slammed down the phone, satisfied she had sufficiently terrified whoever I was talking with. My mom and sister continued to yell at me for talking on the phone with an adult man. And just like the day my dad and aunt saw me wearing a spaghetti strap shirt, they made me feel ashamed and wrong for even talking with Arnold.

"What were you thinking, talking to an adult man on the phone like that?"

"You're disgusting!"

"How could you be so stupid?"

Through all of the shaming and screaming, they never once told me *why* talking with Arnold was a bad idea. They didn't tell me I was being unsafe or that it was inappropriate. And honestly, I felt confused. They always talked about me marrying an older man, so why was it a big deal that I was talking to one? I assumed the problem must have been that I wasn't allowed to talk to boys yet, not that I was talking with an adult. I thought they were mad because I was breaking the rules, not because I was putting myself in danger. Regardless, I retreated to my room, feeling embarrassed and distraught.

For the rest of the night, my mom and sister acted completely normal. They didn't tell my father what happened and instructed me not to tell him either. It was as though I had imagined it all. Unable to articulate my confused mess of emotions, I did what I did best: I kept quiet and stayed in my room as much as I could. But before bed that night, my mom came to me in private.

"Tell me more about this man," she said.

A spark of hope lit up within me, "Mom, he's great! He's a P.E. teacher at my school. He's so nice! He lets me help him around his office, and he is so fun to talk to. He's even got a boat! He's so handsome, and he makes me feel really special and pretty. He makes me really happy, Mom. He likes me, and I like him too. You'd like him, I promise. He lets me come to him and talk about my problems, and he really listens. He really cares about me."

My mom nodded, her face thoughtful. "He has a boat? So he's rich? And teachers get paid well, don't they?"

I shrugged. I had no idea.

She took a moment to think, and then she finally said, "I think it's okay if you keep talking with him. Who knows what will happen as you get older and become a woman? Just keep this between us. Don't tell your sister or your father. Do you understand?"

I nodded.

"Now why don't you call him and tell him that it's okay to keep talking. I'm sure your sister scared him half to death."

I quickly picked up the phone and dialed Arnold's number. Unsurprisingly, he was hesitant to answer, and when he heard me on the other line, he kept trying to get me off the phone.

"Cindy, it's over. Your family knows, and they're gonna call the cops on me if we keep talking. I told you it'd be bad if anyone found out! We can't talk on the phone anymore, okay? Don't call here again."

"Wait!" I interjected. "My mom said it's okay!"

He was silent for a moment. "Are you serious?"

"Yes! She's right here. She said it's okay for us to keep talking. Seriously."

"Put her on the phone."

I gave the phone to my mom and she told him she was okay with us continuing to talk. Her English was choppy, but hearing her give Arnold the green light to continue talking was all he needed.

It's a hard moment to process. My sister was so angry and clearly thought I was an idiot for talking with an adult, but my mom ultimately thought it was okay to keep conversing with him. At the back of my mind, the comments from my friend and my teacher about Arnold being creepy gnawed at me, but if my own mother didn't seem worried, then it was okay, right?

Of course, my mom didn't know the whole story. In her mind, this was a potential opportunity to get her daughter in with a rich man who could take care of me—and her. I'm sure she picked up on the fact that I liked him and thought that he had romantic feelings toward me, but I think she assumed it was just a teenage crush that might evolve into something better when I got older. Regardless of what she thought, her consent was a signal that I wasn't putting myself in harm's way or doing anything wrong. I was just opening the door when opportunity knocked.

So, with my mother's blessing, I defaulted to what I was always taught: don't make a fuss, don't rock the boat, do what you're told. It didn't really matter what I was thinking or feeling at that point. A teacher wanted to invest in me, and my mother thought it was a good idea to see how far that could take me. I just needed to keep quiet and move forward, so that's exactly what I did.

Even with my mother's blessing, everything in me screamed that this was wrong, but I couldn't let myself fully latch on to that feeling. The same cycle of thoughts circled around my head: My mom wasn't worried; Mr. Arnold was a teacher; I was just being dramatic, like always. When had my instincts ever been right before? I told myself I just needed to calm down. I shouldn't cause a fuss when the situation was perfectly normal. And so the wheel turned. Whenever something would happen that didn't sit right, the memory of my mom giving her blessing or Mr. Arnold telling me this was all normal would stifle any urge to speak out. I was slowly buried under a blanket of fear and shame so thick I couldn't see a way out.

Still, I knew I didn't just want to be his go-to person for phone sex.

I did really like talking to him about my life, and I missed that part of our friendship. When he immediately tried to steer the conversation toward phone sex by telling me all of the sexual things he wanted to do with me, I grew brave enough to say, "Is that all you want from me? Why do you want to do those things?" This prompted his asking me if I really loved him and reassuring me that sex wasn't all he wanted from me. This made me feel guilty, so I told him that I loved him because he made me feel secure and valued, hoping he'd want to focus more on that. Sometimes he got the message, backed down, and asked me about my day and how I was feeling.

He liked to talk about the future, which I also liked. I didn't enjoy my homelife, so he kept telling me that he wanted me to come live on his boat with him so I could finish school but be with him until I was old enough for us to marry. It helped me silence those worries I felt about the phone sex and our interaction in the storage room. I told myself he really did care about me, and just like my mom hoped, he had plans to take care of me well into adulthood.

But that wasn't the end of the explicit conversations, and he even started talking about my body as if it were something he had any sort of say over. One day he asked me if I would get a boob job. His question made me feel like I had been punched in the gut. Before this, he had assured me my boobs would come in one day and that he liked how I looked. But now he wanted me to get a boob job?

He must have sensed my discomfort with his comment, because he quickly backtracked, saying, "I mean, you're beautiful, but think about how much more beautiful you'd be with bigger boobs! You've always said you wished they were bigger, haven't you?"

I told him I wasn't sure if I could get a boob job because of money and my parents' opinions. But I couldn't help wondering if the size of my chest, as well as the other areas in which I felt I was physically lacking, would one day drive away this nice man who cared for me. An even smaller, quieter voice made me wonder if those comments were revealing the truth about Kip Arnold—that he was far from the kind-hearted man I thought he was. If he was going back on his comments about my chest, had he been lying to me the entire time about everything? He didn't mention a boob job again, so I tried to forget about it and move forward. I thought if I could keep getting to know him and building trust between us, we'd hit our stride as I got older, and I'd feel more comfortable and adjust to our dynamic. Plus, he continued to be a safe place for me, and whenever I started to doubt him, he reminded me of all his great qualities. He would say something profoundly kind, offer helpful insight into a problem, or promise me that he would always be there when I needed him.

In the summer of 2005, before I started high school, he was there for me in ways no one else was. I remember crying on the phone with him after a particularly nasty fight with my father. In addition to a lot of other awful things, my dad had told me I was worthless and wouldn't amount to anything. His words hurt me incredibly deeply and shook my self-worth to the core. But when I told Arnold what my dad had said and how I was feeling, he shut down my negative self-talk immediately. He was furious with my dad for saying such hurtful things, and he kept insisting that I was great, smart, and had a promising future ahead of me. Then, he told me how much he had missed me since school ended. And regardless of everything that had happened between us, I felt like I might miss him too.

He was quick to let me know that we couldn't be seen together in public; it was too risky. So he said that if we wanted to spend time together outside of school, we'd have to get creative. When he told me that he reserved a hotel room within walking distance of my house, I assumed he just wanted to hang out with me a bit—watch a movie, get a pizza, and just talk. We set up a time to meet at his hotel room when my mom would be at work. My mom didn't end up leaving when I thought she would, so Arnold told me to lie to her. I told my mom I was heading to my cousins' house but went to his hotel instead. Usually, my mom didn't check up on me when I was at my cousins' house, so I knew it would be a safe lie. He told me to be sure I avoided the front office and any hotel staff so that no one saw me come to his room.

When I got there, however, I quickly realized this wasn't about to be a chill hang-out. The room was dark and the curtains were drawn. He looked at me with the same intensity—the same predatory stares—that I had seen in the storage room. As he slowly walked toward me, my heart started to pound. He immediately started touching me, pushing me against the wall, putting his hands up my blouse, and kissing my neck. He kept a firm grasp on me the entire time, but it still felt like he was completely out of control, driven totally by lust and instinct. It was a dichotomy that made me more scared than I had ever been. Something about him holding me like that, and my knowing that his desire was so strong that he couldn't even control it, made every fiber of my being scream "Danger!"

I was trapped. I couldn't physically overpower him if I tried, and I didn't want to hurt his feelings by pushing him away. All I could do was endure it. However, before I understood what was happening, he began to undress me and led me over to the bed. My stomach dropped as I realized he was probably going to try to act out some of the stuff we talked about on the phone. I had no idea what to do next. Was this okay? Why did I feel so scared? He always told me it was normal to feel nervous, but this didn't really feel like regular nerves to me. It felt like I was staring down the barrel of a gun or looking into the eyes of a feral mountain lion that was ready to pounce.

I desperately wanted to stop, to put my clothes on and leave. I started feeling shaky, like I needed to cry, but the aggressive look in his eyes made me too afraid to ask him to slow down. He laid me on the bed and began to perform oral sex on me. I instinctually tensed up and closed my legs, but he told me to relax and let him continue. I closed my eyes and tried to tell myself to chill out. He had talked about oral sex on the phone before; he told me it was good and that it would make me feel good. But all it made me feel was terrified, violated, and sick.

Finally, I decided I couldn't keep going. In spite of my fear of upsetting him or creating problems for no good reason, I spoke up. I told him I was feeling overwhelmed and that it was all too much too fast, and I asked him if it was okay if we took a break. Of course, he wasn't interested in slowing down, so he ignored my concerns and told me I just needed to relax. I felt hopeless. This seemed so wrong, and I wasn't having a good time. I was scared and ashamed. And amidst all the confusion, part of me was frustrated with myself for having such a hard time with everything. He had told me time and again how normal this was for couples to do together. Why was I being such a bummer? Why couldn't I just do as I was told? Why did I have to be like this?

I think he could tell oral sex was just too much, so he switched to fingering me. But instead of helping me to "chill out," this new act only made my anxiety spike, and the feeling of someone's fingers on me and inside of me was terrifying. As he got more intense, the feeling began to morph from uneasiness and discomfort to fear and real physical pain, sending my brain into an entirely different stratosphere. If this was something couples who loved each other did, why was it hurting? It shouldn't hurt, should it? I trusted Arnold. When I tried to tell him it was hurting, he wouldn't stop. I began to panic. He didn't care. He was hurting me, and it didn't matter. Was that because it was supposed to hurt? Even so, why didn't he seem to mind hurting me?

Everything in me wanted to run as far away from him as possible, but I didn't know how I could even begin to leave. Not only did I still not want to hurt his feelings, but his lack of concern over causing me physical pain started to make me worry about what would happen if I upset him. I continued tensing up, despite him telling me to relax, but it only made the pain worse. Ultimately, he got frustrated and decided to change tactics once again. He grabbed a condom and put it on.

He got on top of me with his big body, pinning me to the bed, and I saw the intense determination in his eyes and the sweat that drenched his face. I was so relieved he had stopped touching me, but that relief soon evaporated as he violently tried to penetrate me vaginally. I was trapped. I wanted him to stop, and he was hurting me even worse than before. My heart beat rapidly as he continued to try to penetrate me unsuccessfully. I didn't just feel a little scared anymore. I was terrified. I didn't just feel like I needed to cry; the tears gushed out in desperate sobs. With every one of his attempts to penetrate me, my body was hit with a shock of pain unlike anything I had ever felt before. I felt like he had to be breaking something in me, and I half expected to look down and see that I was lying in a pool of my own blood. Although I cried out in pain and begged him to stop because it hurt, he kept going. He *did not* care. He wanted something, and he was going to take it, no matter how I felt about it.

For the first time ever, Kip Arnold utterly horrified me. I was in agony, and this man that I was supposed to be able to trust was unconcerned. In that moment, I was able to clear out the fog in my mind and see Kip Arnold for who he really was. Maybe I didn't know what a predator was, but I knew this much: he was dangerous. The cautionary words of Mr. Valdemar and my friend's comments about Mr. Arnold being "creepy" rang in my ears. Did they know he was capable of this? Is this what they were trying to warn me about? Did they think this would happen to me if I kept spending time with him? Why didn't they try to talk to me about him again? I blinked the tears out of my eyes as I tried to focus on just surviving the moment and getting out of there.

He let out a frustrated grunt as he realized he was simply not going to be able to penetrate me, so he finally stopped. But before I had a chance to breathe a sigh of relief or make sure I wasn't injured, he demanded I give him a blow job. I knew what it was from our phone calls, but I had never done it before, so he gave me detailed instructions on what to do. When he finally finished, I was in a complete daze. I had no idea how I was supposed to feel. The clarity I experienced just moments before was replaced as fog settled back into my brain, shrouding me in a new cloak of confusion and fear. The intensity of the shock, fear, pain, and confusion made my stomach churn. I wanted to throw up, to get rid of all the nasty feelings, to pretend none of it had happened.

I looked up at him to see his face scrunched up in frustration. I could tell he didn't get exactly what he wanted out of me that day, and he wasn't trying to hide his disappointment. I didn't know if I should feel bad about that, so I just tacked that onto the big mess of horrific emotions pulsing through my veins. I assumed he would ask me what I thought of the entire interaction like he did after our first kiss, so I tried to figure out how I wanted to respond to him. Unlike in the storage room, he didn't ask me how I was or if I enjoyed myself—probably because my tear-stained face was a pretty clear answer. Instead, he made it clear that he wanted me to leave right away and that he was done with me since he got what he wanted (mostly, anyway). I was startled by his sudden coldness and wanted to talk about how I was feeling with someone, though I wasn't sure who I was supposed to talk to after realizing Arnold wasn't a safe option anymore. So, I dressed quickly and left.

As I made my way home, I tried to make sense of what had happened. If this was how couples were supposed to act when they loved each other, why did it hurt so much? Why did it scare me so much? Why did I feel like I wanted to cry, throw up, and scratch my skin off at the same time? Was this how I was supposed to feel? What happened to the man who made me feel special, safe, and loved? How could this be the same guy who comforted me when my dad told me I was worthless? Because, if I was honest, that was how I felt in that moment. Worthless.

CHAPTER THREE
DAMAGED GOODS

It's always disconcerting to see the world around you seem so normal when your reality has been absolutely rocked. I've heard people talk about this when they lose a loved one. Their own lives have suddenly turned gray and lifeless, while everyone around them seems to be moving on—going to movies, buying groceries, telling jokes, and cooking dinner like normal. As I headed home from the hotel, I experienced that same sort of disconnect. Everything felt a little more sinister, like the whole world was mocking me. I wanted to become entirely invisible, and I thought anyone who saw me would immediately know what had just happened, as if I was wearing a big sign around my neck that warned: "*Caution!* Damaged goods!"

As I stumbled home in a daze, trying to sort out what happened, I saw my sister's car in the distance. I quickly ducked behind another car as she drove past. I crouched, hoping she hadn't seen me, then raised my head slightly to see who was inside the car. It was my mom and sister. I could tell from their worried looks, and the way their heads were darting here and there, that they were looking for something. My stomach dropped as I realized that *something* was me. Honestly, if the entire situation hadn't been so horrific, it would have been kind of funny. I went to my cousins' house all the time, and my mom never checked on me. Of course, this would be the *one* time my mom decided to show some interest.

The car drove out of sight, and I dashed home as quickly as I could. My desperate need to concoct some sort of excuse for my mom momentarily trumped the fear and terror of what Arnold did to me in the hotel room. When I saw my sister's car pull up, I did my best to steel myself and put on a brave face. As they entered and saw me, I nodded nonchalantly, trying to conjure up a small smile in greeting.

"Where have you been?!" my mother fumed. "You said you'd be with your cousins! You lied! Where have you been? We've been looking all over for you!"

I shook my head as my brain went into overdrive, searching for some kind of alibi. Would she care if I told her I had been hanging out with Arnold? At the very least, she'd be pissed off that I lied. Arnold had told me to keep the hotel a secret, but he said the same thing about the phone calls, and she didn't seem to mind that. Still, the fear and shame washing over me made me less than eager to open up about my time with Arnold. Maybe she wouldn't have minded if Arnold and I hung out, but I felt too upset and violated to entertain the idea that she'd be on board with what occurred in that hotel room.

So, instead of feeling like I should tell my mom what happened or call out for help, I thought of the arguments I'd had with both her and my father—all their criticisms of me. *I was disgusting for wearing spaghetti straps. If I tried to wear makeup, I was a slut. I was ugly because of my teeth and my nose. I was too much. I made everyone tired. I was worthless. I made bad choices.* Those memories were enough to keep me quiet. I knew that, even if my mother disapproved of what had happened, she wouldn't be coming to my defense any time soon. In her eyes, I would be the one at fault. And at that moment, I didn't have any reason to doubt the truth of that assumption. Maybe it was my fault for leading Arnold on, not being prepared, putting myself in a situation I wasn't ready for, or just my fault for being a slut. There was no way I could tell her, so I tossed out the first lie I could think of.

"No, I told you I wasn't going to be with my cousins. I was hanging out with friends, remember? I don't know, maybe I got confused when we talked, but call Emily; I've been with her all day."

My mother glared at me. I could tell she was trying to decide whether she believed me or not, and I did my best to maintain my poker face. I'm not sure if she was just exhausted or didn't think it was worth the fight, but she believed me. Or she let me go, at the very least. To be safe, I secretly called Emily and asked her to tell my mom I had been with her all day, and she agreed. Arnold was worried my mom would find out, but I assured him that Emily would cover for me. And she did, though I never told her the truth about what she was actually covering up.

When I finally got back to the safety of my room, I tried to unpack what occurred that night. I took a shower, hoping to wash off the feeling of his hands and his body on my skin. Arnold assured me on multiple occasions that this was simply how two people in love acted and that I was more than ready for that type of interaction because I was so mature. If I wasn't so sheltered, I'd know that. Heck, if I wasn't so sheltered, I probably would already have experience with the stuff he tried to get me to do in that hotel room, right?

In spite of my attempts at rationalizing, I couldn't ignore how scared and violated I felt. Maybe this was just what people did, but shouldn't he have listened to me when I asked him to stop or told him he was hurting me? Shouldn't he have cared even a little bit about how I felt after everything was over? Surely it wasn't normal for two people who were supposedly in love—or, at the very least, cared about one another—to have such a scary, almost violent, encounter, and one of the partners to just shoo the other out of the room. Right?

The hardest part was reconciling that sense of betrayal. Sure, Arnold had crossed boundaries before our hotel meeting—a lot of them, honestly—and he acted in ways that now, as an adult, I can say were completely and wholly inappropriate. But before that encounter, he made me feel so safe, so important, so cared about. His attention was meeting a need I didn't even realize my lonely heart was searching to fulfill. I thought I was hanging out with a cool teacher and maybe had a little crush on him, but looking back, it is clear that he was intentionally and tactfully stepping into an almost parental role to gain my trust. He saw how lonely and sad I was; he saw how I wished I could be closer to my parents, even though I didn't know how to say it—and he used these observations as a way to win my trust and affection so he could take full advantage of me. Even though I didn't have the hindsight or emotional maturity to articulate all of that right after our meeting in the hotel room, I instinctively knew he had tricked me. I had never experienced that kind of betrayal before, especially from someone I once viewed as a safe haven.

Kip Arnold took my innocence that day. This is a phrase that gets tossed around a lot, especially when people talk about rape, so you might not understand what I mean when I say that. When I say innocence, I'm not using it as a euphemism for my virginity or level of sexual experience. I mean that he stole the innocent way I viewed the world. He built my trust and shattered it. He made me vulnerable and used that vulnerability to attack. He caused me to question everything I had been told. He made me feel like there was something inherently wrong with me; I began to doubt my instincts, myself, him, and everyone else around me all at once. If I had been lonely before the hotel room, then I was adrift now, floating by myself in the middle of an endless ocean. The world around me looked a lot darker after that night; the way I saw myself and others was tinged with a layer of skepticism and mistrust from then on.

I wish I could tell you that was the last time I ever saw him. I wish I could tell you I ultimately went to my parents, told them what happened, and they ran him out of town on a rail and threw his ass in jail for the rest of his life.

But that's not what happened.

The thing people don't realize about abusers who groom their victims is that they are master manipulators. They are expertly skilled at identifying needs in their victim's lives, exploiting them, and convincing the victim that only the abuser could ever make them happy or love them. And damn it, if Arnold didn't do that exact thing to me.

The crazy thing, which is so difficult to understand, is that regardless of how frightened of him I was after that incident, he still had me firmly in his grasp. He wielded my guilt like a weapon. The way I saw him completely changed, too. He went from a nice, safe man to a creature more like a spider—he was quiet, invasive, could hide effortlessly, and the threat of his presence was easy to miss until he was too close to escape. Because of how smoothly he crept into my life, he was able to manipulate me without much resistance in spite of how he treated me. I definitely didn't trust him, so I tried to keep my eye on him and maintain a healthy space between us, just like you might do when you try to avoid a spider you spot scuttling about in a corner on the ceiling. And keeping that distance was easier to do since I was entering high school and we weren't in the same school building every day.

But Arnold had done such an expert job of twisting my mind that I didn't trust myself or my instincts. Because I believed I had to closely guard the secret of what had happened between us, he was the only person I could be totally and completely honest with. He had me fully convinced that no one could ever know me or understand me like he did. I didn't feel like it was right to cause a fuss by speaking out, even if I had been sexually assaulted. Plus, my parents had already done a great job of making me feel like I was morally bankrupt no matter what I did. I was certain that if this were to get out, I would be vilified as the girl who was too much of a slut to stop her teacher from trying to have sex with her.

Still, I knew I didn't like what happened at the hotel. I knew I felt degraded and dehumanized by his actions, but I don't think I could have vocalized then that he raped or attacked me. I just knew I didn't like what he did, and every ounce of me wanted to get as far from him as possible. But he wasn't ready to loosen his grip on me just yet. He called me almost every day, and the night after he violated me, he wanted me to talk to him about it. When I left the hotel room, I could tell he was frustrated that he wasn't able to have vaginal sex with me, but the way he talked on the phone, it was clear that he was still stoked about what he had done to me.

And if my terrified sobs hadn't been a clear enough indication, my coldness on the phone let him know that I wasn't on board with any of it. I wasn't shy about letting him know that I hadn't enjoyed it and did not want it to happen again—ever. At that point, he started to work overtime to convince me I didn't understand how adults expressed their love to one another and to guilt me into believing that I was mean and judged him for being overweight. Again and again, Arnold recounted what he did to me that day, how I looked to him, and how it felt for him. He constantly tried to reassure me that everything we did was perfectly normal and good. Although my whole body screamed "danger," the deep-seated cycle of self-doubt rattled my resolve, and I knew I could never tell him to go away. If my mom thought it was a good thing to talk to him, I must be wrong about feeling weird about him, right? And so, the wheel turned.

I kept talking to him, all while trying my best to put up boundaries between us. I let him know I wasn't happy about what he did at the hotel without totally putting him off, and I tried to steer our conversations toward the non-sexual realms. It seemed to work. I started high school, and he kept working at the middle school. Because he was so worried about being seen in public with a kid, I only had to deal with his incessant explicit phone calls. *I can handle that*, I thought.

But he soon started keeping tabs on me in other ways. When I walked to school, he drove past, watching me. He even offered to give me a ride and occasionally tried to touch me or kiss me. He became ever more like that sneaking spider, constantly creeping around corners and always popping up when you thought you had finally evaded him.

A few months after he raped me, he invited me to another hotel room. For whatever reason, I agreed. I guess I just didn't want to upset him, and to be honest, at that point I felt too scared to tell him no. If he was capable of hurting me like he did the first time, I had no idea how he might respond if I really upset him. And every time I thought about saying no to him, I recalled that look in his eyes moments before he attacked me in the hotel room and in the storage closet—like he was hunting me. It was a look of feral determination that chilled me to the bone, and even though I didn't totally understand it, I instinctually knew I should tread carefully.

Plus, I had been constantly fed the idea that my gut instincts were wrong, not only by Arnold as he groomed me but also by my parents. Whenever I did something they didn't like—even if it wasn't inherently against the rules—they came down on me, hard. Their control wasn't limited to the realm of my appearance, such as makeup or clothes. It also extended to my free time. I was still finding my footing as a freshman in high school, but I wasn't able to go out of the house much beyond school, occasional library trips, and quick errands to the CVS down the street. I was just on the precipice of being able to make my own choices about my future, explore new interests, and decide how I wanted to spend my free time.

However, at every turn, my parents made me feel like I would only make bad choices, so they kept me under their careful watch as often as possible. If I wanted to meet a friend, let alone a boy, my mom told me I was safer at home. In this context, when my mom actively consented to my talking to Arnold, I thought that this was one thing I was actually *allowed* to do. Maybe I needed to follow her advice and ignore the pit in my stomach. Besides, there wasn't anyone else with whom I could share my feelings after a big fight with my parents. Even with how scary, degrading, and violent the attack in the hotel was for me, Arnold was always quick to compliment me. He often told me I was smart, I had value, and that my ideas were good.

So with all of that fogging my brain, I agreed to meet him in another hotel room. This time, instead of choosing a hotel within walking distance of my house, Arnold told me to meet him outside of a restaurant near my school. He said he would pick me up and drive me to the hotel room he'd gotten for us. I agreed, and when the day and meeting time came around, I hopped into his car. I don't know if he picked a hotel located farther away because he wanted to have a bit more control over me and the situation, but this time he reserved a room in a different city. I know now that the hotel wasn't too far from my house, but at the time, it seemed like I was basically on a different planet—and the isolation added to my fear. The idea of enduring a repeat of what had happened the last time, and in a place that felt so far away from anything familiar, filled me with sickening dread.

Somehow, I found the guts to tell him I didn't want to do anything sexual in that hotel. I said I wanted to hang out, maybe watch a movie or something, but I didn't want to get physical. He was disappointed and admitted he wasn't expecting to just hang out. He looked grief-stricken and asked if he disgusted me. Not wanting to upset him, I lied and told him he did not. Still, I insisted that I didn't want anything physical to happen. Maybe it was because he had only just started to tread into getting physical with me, or maybe he was surprised at my sudden strength, but Arnold agreed. He made sure I knew how annoyed he was—huffing, puffing, and pouting the entire time we were together—but that second time in the hotel room we just hung out, had some food, and watched TV.

Arnold changed his approach once he realized I was starting to stand up for myself. Instead of trying to convince me that the attack in the hotel room was normal and an act for two people in love, he switched to guilt-tripping. When I tried to steer him away from sexual conversations or was evidently upset or cold with him, he made me feel like the worst person in the world. Arnold was overweight, and whenever I refused to respond to something sexual in enthusiastic terms, he insinuated that it was because of his weight, saying I must be tired of being with someone fat and would find someone younger and thinner.

"You're embarrassed to be with me, aren't you? You think my body is disgusting. I know you think I'm gross. You just want to be with someone sexier. You care so much about looks that you can't see how much I care about you. You're just using me, aren't you?"

I couldn't believe myself. Here was a man who was simply trying to show me he loved me and could potentially take care of my family and me for the rest of our lives, and I was pushing him away? He made himself vulnerable for me, and I just met him with coldness? He was only trying to treat me like any other boyfriend might treat his girlfriend. He wasn't treating me as if I was an ignorant kid like everyone else did. He saw that I was different from the other teenage girls, and he wanted to express that love in a physical way too. I hadn't told anyone how far things had gotten with Arnold, and my friends didn't suspect anything was wrong with me. Because I didn't have anyone with whom I could talk through the situation, I just assumed the problem was me. Why couldn't I just be nice to him? Why couldn't I just return his affections? What was wrong with me?

So I tried to be nicer. I told him about my day. I talked to him about school. Sometimes he even asked me about guys at school, and whether I had a crush on anyone. I wasn't too worried about that, as he had asked me if I cared if he had sex with other women since he couldn't regularly be with me. Not understanding what he was asking, I told him that was fine. So, when he asked about boys at school, I chalked it up to him understanding the reality of our situation and maybe being more on board with some healthy distance between the two of us. I thought that maybe I wouldn't have to be physical with him anymore. I was being totally honest when I told him there wasn't anyone in particular that I was crushing on.

And then I met Juan.

I know you're probably expecting me to tell you a romantic story about how we locked eyes at a school dance or something and the entire room fell away around us. In reality, the first time I really remember interacting with Juan was in the lunchroom, and I thought he was super weird. I sat on the side of the cafeteria we called "the dark side" because it was noticeably darker than the rest of the cafeteria. Of course it wasn't really darker;

it just looked that way because the punks and goths sat there, so everyone was decked out in all black. Meanwhile, Juan typically sat with the preppy kids. Even though we were on different sides of the cafeteria, he had a really bad habit of staring at me like a total creeper. To his credit, I'm sure I stood out. While my friends were into the punk rock, sort-of goth look, it wasn't really my thing. I was pretty easy to spot in the lunchroom, as I was the only one sitting on the dark side wearing light blue jeans and cute, colorful tops. But still, I wasn't sure how to process the attention I got from Juan. Did he not like me? Did he think I looked funny? Did he like me? Had we met before? I wasn't sure, but after far too much meaningful eye contact for my taste, I wrote him off as the weird new kid from the preppy lunch table.

But everything changed one day when Juan wasn't able to find a seat at his usual table, so he had to come over to the dark side. Of course, this was high school, so instead of striking up a conversation with me, Juan did what any smart high schooler would do: he sent his buddy over to talk to me. The plan was for this guy to act as Juan's wingman. He'd gauge my interest in Juan, try to talk him up to me, and see if I would be up for talking with Juan or even going on a date with him—a foolproof plan!

What actually happened was that Juan's buddy abandoned the plan somewhere between leaving Juan and talking to me. He made his own master plan and decided to start putting the moves on me for himself. And since I didn't know the backstory with Juan, I figured there wasn't any harm with going out with him. Shockingly, our romance was a short-lived one, as I realized he was a total goober. It didn't take me long to tell him I wasn't into it and move on. Vindicated, Juan took that as his opportunity to move in. He started talking to me himself, and despite the weirdness of our first interactions, I realized that I really liked talking to him.

Juan was silly and could make me laugh unlike anyone else. I had fun when we were together, and I could tell that he genuinely cared about getting to know me more simply because he liked me as a person—not because he was trying to get something from me. The more time we spent together, the more I could feel myself falling for him. It was the quintessence of a high school romance. We were kids, slowly falling for one another, both equally awkward and inexperienced but both trying our best to figure out what to do with our growing feelings for each other.

And then I went home and fielded calls from the middle school teacher who had assaulted me when I was fourteen.

My dynamic with Arnold had shifted significantly. I was a sophomore in high school, and we hadn't really met up in person since Arnold booked the second hotel room. Even though Arnold did like to talk about sexual stuff on the phone, he spent a lot of time talking to me like a friend. He seemed genuinely curious when he asked if I was crushing on a boy, and the more we talked, the more our interactions seemed to build into a kind of strange friendship. Of course, I didn't clock that his increased interest in me and my daily life in high school was a new way to groom me, understand my schedule, and find ways to control me. I just thought he was chilling out, settling back into the role of a friend or mentor.

Eventually, I told him about Juan. I was excited to tell Arnold about this boy I was falling for. Juan was funny, nice, treated me well, and we had so much in common. Being with him was fun and effortless, and he was such a breath of fresh air in my life. I was certain my good friend Kip Arnold would be excited to hear about such a great, positive influence entering my life. When I rang him up and began telling him about Juan, I know you could hear the excitement in my voice—I couldn't help but smile!

But it quickly became clear that Arnold did not share my enthusiasm. He screamed at me; he called me a slut, claimed I was shallow, accused me of two-timing him, and wondered how I could ever think my being with someone like Juan was a good thing. He screamed about how he was going to take care of me, while Juan was just going to break my heart and leave. It seemed like he called Juan and me every awful name he could think of. My joy and excitement were zapped out of me as I sat and listened to his verbal lashing.

My mom actually heard us on the phone that day. She doesn't speak English, so she couldn't understand what we were saying. But she knew that Arnold was mad—and thought it was hilarious. When I hung up, she approached me, laughing.

"What was going on? Was that Arnold? He sounded so angry! He was like a pitbull growling! I could probably have heard him all the way across the room!"

I laughed nervously and shrugged. "Oh, you know how guys get sometimes."

And I left it at that. My mom might have been okay with me talking on the phone with Arnold, but oddly enough, dating Juan would have been totally against the rules. Hanging out with boys and dating were completely out of the question, so the last thing I needed was a lecture from my mother right after getting raked over the coals by a guy I thought was trying to be my friend.

I felt like I was two people. There was the Cindy everyone knew at school, and there was the more cynical, cold Cindy who Arnold would talk to on the phone. Arnold could tell that I had developed quite a crush on Juan and that my feelings were only growing every day. So, after that first initial screaming session, he continued to hound me about Juan. Arnold was not willing to lose me to a kid, so he tried to really drive home the idea that I was damaged goods, and Juan could never want someone who had the history I did.

"So you're really starting to like this Juan kid?"

"I don't know," I said, trying to direct our phone conversation away from him.

I heard him snort in disbelief as he drew out a deep sigh. "You tell him about us yet?" he asked.

"What? Of course not."

"Good. Because you know he'd never want you if he knew about us. About me."

I sighed.

"Cindy, I'm telling you I can take care of you. You're in high school now. Before you know it, you'll be eighteen. I can make you happy. I just need you to stop being so cold with me and so shallow about my looks. I need you to finally decide you're in it for the long haul. Why can't you just love me like I love you?"

"That's not fair."

"No, what's not fair is that you're giving me the runaround for *Chunti* over there at school."

I scoffed at his use of such a racist term, but before I could say anything, he continued, "You keep seeing him, and see what happens. He's gonna crush your heart, or he'll knock you up and leave. Then you'll come running back, ready to have a real relationship with me. And let me tell you, if he ever finds out about me, he's gonna kick you to the curb so fast you won't know what hit you."

There it was. The stakes were made crystal clear. If I wanted Juan, Arnold had to remain a secret. I could never be fully honest with Juan, because if he learned the truth, he'd never look at me the same way. He'd start seeing me like my family did—exhausting, too much, disgusting, and as someone with terrible instincts. Beyond that, how could I ever expect him to trust me and fully love me if he knew what I had done? What high school guy would want any kind of relationship with a girl who had already had all sorts of experience with her middle school gym teacher? Arnold was right. Juan would drop me as soon as he found out the truth.

But I couldn't fight the feelings I had for Juan. I still wasn't able to say with confidence that my experiences with Arnold were abusive, but I knew Juan never made me feel like Arnold did. Almost everything with Arnold felt forced, foreign, and unnatural; it didn't make sense or feel real. The situation with Arnold was upsetting because he was such a great listener. He still managed to make me feel incredibly safe one moment and incredibly vulnerable the next. That inconsistency kept me on my toes, and I held onto him a little tighter because I wasn't sure what Arnold would do if things went sideways. With the fractured foundation of my family and Arnold's malicious grooming and manipulation, I didn't think I could trust my desires and instincts. I was like his puppet, and even though I wasn't happy with my circumstances, I was certain I'd be worthless and alone forever if I made Arnold's abuse public or tried to leave him. And that's a lot for a teenager to process all on her own.

But where things with Arnold were complicated, my relationship with Juan felt totally natural. I remember sitting outside on a curb with Juan. It was a small curb, but we were both able to fit. He told me he should probably keep his distance because he was sick, but I told him he could stick around because I had a cold anyway. If you ask Juan, I was totally flirting with him, and he took it as a green light to move in closer and ultimately give me a kiss on the forehead. I really wasn't trying to flirt, but I'd be lying if I told you it wasn't one of my favorite memories from our early days together. It's also one of the strangest, given what was happening in secret. I had been raped and experienced a ton of sexual things with my teacher, and yet I was inadvertently sending out romantic signals, flirting, and feeling a mixture of shyness and excited butterflies from sitting so close to a boy from school.

It was complicated and confusing, but I knew I couldn't just walk away from someone who made me feel the way Juan did. I only hoped that I could make him love me enough to overlook what had happened with Arnold or make Arnold lose interest and move on.

CHAPTER FOUR
THE STALKER

It wasn't long before my mom found out about Juan. My sister saw us holding hands as we were walking home, and naturally she didn't waste time reporting her findings. My mother said that we had better just be friends and not to tell my father about Juan. With my sister constantly threatening that she would tell my dad, I finally decided to tell him myself. I was prepared for a huge meltdown, but to my surprise my dad laughed. He didn't seem upset at all and quickly asked to meet both Juan and his mom, which completely shocked both Juan and me. At first, my mom liked him too. She still was fine with me talking to Arnold, but Juan seemed to be a nice boy, was respectful, and made me happy, so she was on board with us dating.

But Arnold became furious and often told me it was unfair that Juan got to see me but he couldn't. He began to follow me when I walked to school, and unbeknownst to Juan, Arnold began to follow him as well. If I didn't answer Arnold's calls, he demanded to know whether I had been talking to Juan. Arnold watched my house to see when I was or was not spending time with Juan. He peppered me with questions about where I was, who I was with, and grimly asked me if "Chunti" had been with me. I felt so conflicted when Arnold said I was crazy and just didn't know what I wanted or that I was stringing him along. It was such a stark contrast to the man I had met at fourteen who promised he would always be there for me and made me feel safe and cared for when I fought with my parents.

After a few weeks, it all became too much, so I lied and told him I broke up with Juan.

Unfortunately, that lie didn't stick; a year later, he found out the truth. It was 2007, and I would soon turn seventeen. Arnold casually asked some of his former students about me in an attempt to get the truth. They told him that Juan and I were still very much together. Arnold was furious and called me a "cheater." He demanded to know how I could have betrayed him when he had been faithful to me. I didn't know what to think. It all sounded wrong, but at the same time, guilt washed over me. I could hear how angry and hurt Arnold was, and I knew my actions caused his hurt. Arnold still called himself my boyfriend pretty frequently, though I definitely didn't view him as my boyfriend.

I was disgusted with myself. Disgusted for putting myself in this position. Disgusted for being unfaithful to Juan with Arnold and for being unfaithful to Arnold with Juan. And I felt disgusted that I even thought there was some kind of "relationship" where I could be unfaithful to Arnold. I was certain that I was just a terrible person. And because all of our interactions were secret and happened in the echo chamber of Arnold's lies and gaslighting, I wasn't able to confide in anyone to get a rational perspective on the situation. But one thing became increasingly clear to me: I didn't want to be with Arnold. Even though I felt torn doing it, I told him that maybe it would be best if we were just friends. His response was predictable.

"No. I can't do that, Cindy."

"Why?!" I pleaded. "Let's just be friends. I think this is just too much for both of us. Maybe we aren't good for each other."

"I love you too much to be your friend. I desire you too much. I have to be with you. You have to break up with Juan. This is crazy. I don't deserve this. I can't believe you're two-timing me with Chunti at school. It's time to be an adult, Cindy. Break it off with him. *Now.* This isn't fair. I'm alone; it's just me and my dog living on my boat. I'm doing all of this to be good to you, and you're out all the time with Chunti? You know that's messed up, Cindy. You know you're acting like a slut."

Once again, Arnold had managed to work his twisted, vengeful magic and make me feel like I was in the wrong. But I refused to relent. Instead, I tried to steer our conversations away from Juan. Of course, that wasn't what he wanted. So, when I joined my school's flag team, he saw his opportunity and jumped. He started hanging out during practice and calling himself an assistant coach, however wildly unofficial that title was. He was neither a teacher at my high school nor had he ever coached a girls' flag team. My flag coach knew about it but didn't seem to mind, and Arnold kept the relationship friendly by acting extremely helpful. He brought us food when we had long or late practices. He also helped drive us to events, taking some responsibilities off my coach's plate. All the while, of course, he found every opportunity to be physically close to me. But where Mr. Valdemar had had issues with Arnold taking me out of his P.E. class in eighth grade, my flag coach was pretty apathetic toward Arnold. He didn't seem to have much of a rapport with him, but he also didn't seem to care that Arnold was spending so much time "helping."

Arnold found new ways to wriggle into my life. He bought me a phone so he could call me as frequently as he liked without worrying that the calls would show up on the phone bill my father paid. If I didn't answer his calls, he parked outside of the house and watched. He let me know that he was setting his sights on Juan, and I started to worry what he might do if he was able to corner Juan.

"So, you were hanging out with Chunti last night?"

I sighed. "What are you talking about?"

"I was outside your house last night when you didn't answer my calls. I saw him drive you home."

"You were outside of my *house?*"

"Of course I was. You weren't answering my calls. I was worried. You don't think, Cindy. You're just out at all hours of the night with this kid, and who knows what will happen to you when you do stuff like that?"

"What are you talking about, all hours? I have a curfew! You know that. I was just having fun. It wasn't a big deal."

"You say that now, Cindy, but I'll tell you, you're playing with fire with this Juan kid. You need to drop him. I'm serious."

"Stop."

"He's not good for you. You just don't know it yet, but I do. You need to break things off with him. Stop hurting me; stop doing stuff that's bad for you, and be with me. And if you can't do it, maybe he and I just need to have a talk."

"I don't want you around Juan."

Arnold scoffed, "You don't get it, do you? I'm not just watching you. I'm watching *him*. I've been following him home after your little dates. You hear me? So don't think for a second that you're giving me the slip or that I'm not here, ready to fight for you. I just want you to think about that the next time you're spending time with Chunti. I want you to look out the window or into the parking lot and see me, and maybe one day it will get through your selfish head what you're doing to me—and to yourself. Do you hear me? I'll be around you, and I'll be around him. I'll always be around."

And he meant it. If we were hanging out at a Starbucks and I looked outside, I saw Arnold's car at the end of the parking lot where he watched us. He followed us as we drove places. He showed up at games, and sometimes I even spotted him hiding out at practice in a different car. Even if I didn't immediately notice his car, his 300-plus pound frame was easy to spot. Arnold was everywhere, and I was never quite certain what he was capable of. Since he seemed to always be around, I never felt like I could fully cut things off with him. Once he started to stalk Juan and me, I became more freaked out about what he could do to Juan, my family, or me. And he clearly didn't have any trouble learning my schedule and following me everywhere I went. I wondered what would happen if I made a guy like that angry.

He threatened me nearly every day, promising to tell Juan everything if I didn't dump him on my own. He played to my insecurities about my skin tone by saying that when he saw me with Juan, I looked like "an ordinary Mexican, bound to get pregnant." I quickly shifted into survival mode, trying to keep myself, my boyfriend, and my family safe from this stalker who seemed to be everywhere I turned. It didn't take long for me to become hypervigilant and a bit obsessive. I kept an eye on the street outside of my home to try to spot his car. Every time I was out, I was always looking over my shoulder, covertly trying to see if he was tailing us. I never knew if he would try to run our car off the road, run up to me and Juan on a date and try to hurt Juan, or simply approach us and tell Juan everything. So I always made it my first priority to find him as soon as I headed out.

He started to choose his language very carefully. Before Juan came into my life, Arnold lavished me with compliments. He praised the fact that I was mature, smart, pretty, kind, and special. His tactics shifted though, and he cunningly withheld all compliments, instead peppering me with a barrage of hateful and demeaning comments as a way to entice me to leave Juan and be "faithful" to him. Using a toxic but carefully considered combination of manipulation and fear, he made me doubt every instinct and every thought I had.

Even though the secrets I kept from Juan filled me with guilt, I couldn't leave him. Juan made me feel like no one ever had. He wasn't afraid to goof around, he dreamed big dreams, and more than anything, he wanted to make me happy. He was handsome and fun, and when I thought about the kind of guy I would end up with, it was always someone like Juan—never someone like Kip Arnold. In my mind, I didn't believe I was in a relationship with Arnold, but it still didn't feel right or like I was being entirely faithful to Juan.

As I compared my interactions with Juan and Arnold, I recognized the stark contrast between them. Over time, I was better able to pinpoint the ways Arnold manipulated me. Where Arnold made me feel like I was out of my depth, powerless, ignorant, or pressured, Juan made me feel safe, informed, and like I was a true partner. Arnold had, at one time, made me feel like I finally had a voice, but as soon as I used that voice to say stuff he didn't like, he tried to shut me up again. Juan, on the other hand, wanted to hear my voice to get to know me, even when we didn't agree; he wasn't listening so he could mine for information to figure out ways to manipulate me.

But most telling of all, Juan didn't try to guilt-trip me to get his way, especially when it came to the physical nature of our relationship. The first time Arnold had assaulted me in the storage room at my middle school, I felt hunted and trapped, like being tossed into the ocean without a life jacket. However, with Juan, the physical nature of our relationship grew naturally as we grew closer. Our first kiss was something we both wanted and were both ready for—even though we were both nervous! And we had sex for the first time because we were in love.

Finally, I started to understand how Arnold had taken some truths and twisted them to fit his agenda. He was right that people in love expressed themselves in a physical way, but the way Juan and I were first physically intimate wasn't about making either of us feel hunted or pressured. Of course we were nervous, but not because we were fearful or felt threatened; it was nervous excitement. Juan cared about how I felt throughout, and I cared about how he felt. It was about the two of us coming together and giving each other mutual pleasure, where Arnold was only interested in what he could take from me.

My relationship with Juan was beautiful, and with every passing day, my desire to preserve it and protect him increased. At one time, Arnold may have made me feel safe, but I knew that it was an illusion. Now, Arnold frightened me. I was afraid of what he might do, but I knew I wouldn't let him destroy what I had with Juan without a fight. So, if that meant I had to talk with him on the phone a few times or not care if he parked outside my house, then so be it.

With his relentless cycle of verbal abuse, fear, and love-bombing, Arnold kept me on the hook. I was too afraid to leave, and I still couldn't help but appreciate how good of a listener he was. Even though I loved Juan and he clearly cared for me, I couldn't tell Juan everything. But Arnold knew all of my secrets—mainly because *he* was my biggest, darkest secret. And he used that as ammunition to manipulate and trap me. When Juan's prom came around during my junior year of high school, Arnold started nagging me about buying a prom dress. He called me constantly, insisting that I needed to let him buy my dress.

"C'mon, Cindy, you know how you are. You don't have any fancy dresses like that, and you definitely don't have money to buy one."

I sighed. "It's gonna be fine. I can get myself a nice dress."

"Cindy, I want you to look nice, okay? Can't you just let me take care of you? I know what's going to be best for you. Let me get you a dress."

"I really don't want you to buy me a dress. I'd rather take care of it myself."

"How? You don't have money. Are you going to ask your parents? You know they don't have the money for that. Are you going to really hurt them like that? Put the burden of your silly prom dress on them on top of everything else they've got to worry about? Even *you* aren't that selfish. C'mon, I can get you a dress that would make you look nicer than anything you'd be able to get. I know what looks good. You don't know what looks good. Let me help you."

After days and days of incessant calls like that, I couldn't take it anymore. The reality was, I didn't have the money to buy a dress for prom. Arnold had skillfully picked his words, and even entertaining the thought of putting the financial burden of a prom dress on my parents made me feel terribly selfish. So, after what felt like the millionth call from him about the dress, I finally gave in. He had completely worn me down. So I justified it by telling myself his buying me a dress for Juan's prom had to be a good sign. Maybe he was being truthful when he told me he was just trying to be friends. Maybe he was finally willing to let me go. I didn't love the idea of dress shopping with him, but I also knew I couldn't keep fighting him, so we set a time for Arnold to pick me up.

We went to the mall, and I tried on dresses. It was a surreal and awkward experience, even though an adult buying a kid a dress for a dance isn't inherently strange or necessarily concerning. Of course, it does get a lot weirder when you factor in Arnold not being my parent or guardian; plus, he had assaulted me twice and was constantly threatening and stalking my boyfriend and me. I felt like I was walking on eggshells the whole time we were shopping, treading carefully and trying to act as normal as possible so nothing aroused suspicion. But with every raised eyebrow and every sideways glance, I felt like I was on the edge of cracking and spilling out all the disgusting mess inside.

Each time I tried on a dress, and I liked it but he didn't, he demanded I put it back. And if he liked a dress but I didn't, he made me hang on to it. Any thoughts I had about the look, feel, or fit of the dress didn't matter. He didn't listen to my opinions at all and only acted on what he thought was best. I felt like such a puppet trying on outfits for him—100 percent powerless and voiceless. He didn't want to buy me a prom dress that I liked—he wanted to buy something *he* liked. He made it very clear to me that I just needed to try on the dresses he picked for me and keep quiet if I didn't like something. It was like he was using the dress to create this very physical reminder for me while I was at Juan's prom: *My opinion matters, yours doesn't, and even though you're out with Juan right now, I'm still right there between you two.* Ultimately, we landed on a dress that he liked and I was okay with, and he bought it for me. I insisted that he didn't have to do that, but he told me it was his idea, so he should pay for the dress. I gave up and let him. When we got back into his car, he told me he needed to go home to his boat to grab something.

I didn't think anything of it, so I agreed. I figured he would get what he needed, drive me home, and maybe this would all be over. I hated driving in the car with him, because any time he had me in a car alone, he grabbed whatever he could on my body. It didn't matter what I was doing, how I was acting, or if I was in the middle of talking about something.

He just reached over whenever the mood struck him and shoved his hand down my shirt or between my legs. And this car ride wasn't any different. It was just another reminder that he didn't care what I thought, felt, or wanted. He was frantically grabbing at anything to try to slake his lust. It was exhausting and demeaning, but I knew if I could just get through the car ride, he'd drop me off at home and I could have a moment of peace. When he asked me to come onto his boat with him while he looked for whatever he was missing, I did.

It was the first time I had seen his boat, and I was surprised at how small it was. I don't know if I necessarily expected his boat to be a yacht, but I certainly pictured something a little nicer and a little more spacious than what was essentially a floating studio apartment/bachelor pad. He let me get on before him, and when I turned to watch him, I was struck by how his large frame looked so jammed in the tiny walkway to get below deck. He always loved to brag about his boat. This was what convinced my mother that he was rich and made her okay with us talking. This boat was supposed to be emblematic of how he could take care of me. But when I was there, I saw it for what it really was: small, dirty, and shabby; a space not fit for one person, let alone the two of us.

It was the perfect metaphor for his place in my life. I sat down on one of the small couches, and he sidled around the room, trying to squeeze in the space and near me. I sighed and looked around the room and asked if he had found what he was looking for. He ignored me and immediately started talking about Juan.

"I can't believe you haven't broken up with Chunti yet."

I rolled my eyes. "Don't call him that. And we've talked about this—"

"No," he said, interrupting me. "This is ridiculous. I just bought you a prom dress for *his* prom. This is crazy. If you don't break up with him after prom, I'm telling him everything. It's been too long already. You're lying to him; you're cheating on me. It's not right. You can't treat people this way, Cindy! You've been cheating and lying to me, but I'm still here. I'm sticking it out. I'm a good guy, and you're doing this to me for Chunti? He's not like me. As soon as he hears about what you've been doing, he's gonna be out. He's not going to care. He's going to think you're trash, but I'll still be here."

I looked down at my hands. I didn't know what to say. The guilt was almost unbearable. I hated keeping stuff from Juan, and I felt smothered by Kip Arnold. I was so afraid that he was right, that Juan would dump me the second I was honest about my relationship with Arnold. And who could blame him? I deserved it, didn't I? If I was honest with Juan and we ended up breaking up, Arnold would still be hanging around. The thought horrified me. He would *always* be there. I would never get rid of him, even if I tried to get away on my own. Was there even a way out of this at this point? Would I just have to marry him and live on this awful boat forever?

I swallowed back a lump in my throat as he grabbed my chin and slowly turned me to face him. My heart started pounding and my stomach lurched. I felt like I was going to throw up. My eyes darted frantically around the boat as I tried to find a way out, but there was nowhere to run. He leaned in to start kissing me, then began to touch me all over. I wasn't sure how I felt about everything else in my life, but I knew *this* wasn't what I wanted. I pushed him away.

"Stop it."

His gaze made my blood run cold. He slowly took another step toward me, his stare growing more intense and almost fiery with each step. It was the same look from the storage room and the hotel, amplified times a million. I was torn between sheer terror because of what was about to happen and anger with myself for walking into what was obviously a trap. Waves of fear and nausea simultaneously racked my body as I tried to figure out what would happen to me. By the look in his eyes, I could tell my feelings were inconsequential. He wanted something from me. The words he spoke to me in the P.E. office all those years ago rang through my head: *I want everything from you.* And slowly, he was taking everything from me. My innocence. My independence. My needs. My feelings. My safety. My security. Over the years, he had gradually chipped away at me, and I was always too ashamed and scared to call out for help.

Before I could say anything, he said, "I'm going to take what's mine. I've waited too long, and you're going to be mine."

My heart felt like it would beat right out of my chest, and my breath puffed out in panicked gasps. I didn't know how to stop him. His body was blocking the way off the boat, and I knew screaming wouldn't do any good. The harbor where Arnold docked his boat had a constant stream of people coming in and out, so even though it wasn't an exceptionally noisy, touristy place like Santa Monica Pier, it was busy enough to keep someone from hearing my screams. And even if someone did manage to hear me, by the time they could figure out which boat the screams were coming from, who knows what Arnold could have done to me by then? All at once, I felt too hot and too cold as my fight or flight response sent all of my senses into overdrive to get me out of his reach. But I couldn't get away, so I stood up, raised my arms defensively, and said as firmly and powerfully as I could, "No."

He batted my arms away and said, "Stop playing games." Then, he pushed me down on the couch, pulling my clothes off my body.

The feeling of him on top of me nauseated me, and tears started streaming down my face. I wanted to rip off my skin to get rid of the sickening sensation of his hands on my skin, up my blouse, between my legs. I wished I could snap my fingers and disappear or burst into flames and turn him into a smoldering pile of ash along with me. But I knew I wouldn't be able to fight him off. My desperate pleas for him to stop fell on deaf ears. Ultimately, he removed my pants, even as I tried to push him away from me.

He shook his head and said, "Cindy, don't fight it. Your mind is telling you no, but your body is telling you yes!"

I didn't scream—what was the point? I was totally on my own, helpless and overpowered. All I could do was keep pushing his giant frame away from me, pleading with him through the tears to stop. After all, I remembered in the hotel that he became frustrated with the resistance and ultimately switched tactics. Maybe the same thing would happen, and I could get away somehow. But he kept repeating that he was going to take what was his, and he abruptly turned me on my stomach. Before I could even process what was happening, he was anally raping me.

My body exploded in pain and I cried out, begging him to stop. But he didn't. It was as if I wasn't even in the room anymore. Wholly focused on getting what he wanted, he ruthlessly pounded his body against mine until he finally finished; all the while I sobbed, still trying to push him away however I could. When it was all over, I laid still for a moment like a ragdoll, overcome with pain, horror, shock, fear, and disbelief. He didn't ask how I was feeling. He didn't care. It was clear in his eyes that he felt like he had won the lotto. He finally got what we wanted from me.

It was the most terrifying look I had ever seen in a man's eyes. He wasn't happy that we had finally consummated a relationship, he wasn't feeling "closer to me than ever," and he wasn't feeling overcome with love. He had the look of a conqueror in his eyes. He wanted something from me that I kept from him for years, and he finally took it. As far as he knew, he had conquered me. Despite my best efforts to remove him from my life, he got me alone, overpowered me, and raped me. Again. First the hotel room, and now this. I hadn't been able to do a thing to stop him. He was certain he had won. And I was terrified that he had too.

During the entire car ride back to my house, he was practically bursting with joy. It was obvious that he believed he finally got something he deserved, and he wasn't about to let anything dampen his mood. Not even the silent shell of a girl beside him. I didn't say a word, as I couldn't stop berating myself for letting something like this happen. When I finally arrived at home, I got out of Arnold's car slowly and walked to my bathroom to shower. As the water rushed over me, I felt horrified and disgusted with myself. I was a liar. A slut. How could I have let this happen to me? Why didn't I fight him more? Why didn't I yell? Why didn't I try to run? Sure, when I did try to push him, it didn't even budge his 300-plus pound frame, but couldn't I have kept trying?! *Maybe I asked for this to happen to me*, I thought.

I was furious with myself. How could I cheat on Juan? I had so hoped the dress would be an exit ramp from Arnold's involvement in my life, but I realized I was just digging myself deeper into a hole. I was trapped, and I didn't see a way out. Through it all, I couldn't bear the thought of losing Juan, but I also didn't see how I could keep him in my life after what happened.

Even worse, Arnold was around a lot more than I wanted. Not only did his stalking behavior increase, but with his new role on my flag team and my growing older, he became more comfortable being seen with me in public. He even started to drive me to competitions. His unofficial assistant-coach status for my flag team meant he could get a ton of direct access to me. This gave him plenty of opportunities for alone time when he could continue to manipulate me, scare me, and grab me whenever he wanted. I felt like I was drowning, and no one even knew I was in the water.

The way he spoke to me became more alarming too. When he tried to bring up the rape on the boat—of course he never called it rape and always spoke of it as if everything was consensual—I attempted to move to another topic. It had been clear on my tear-streaked face at the time, and I made it clear on the phone calls afterward, that I had not enjoyed it and that infuriated him. One day, it got to be too much, and he gave me a glimpse of a new corner of his dark soul.

"I know that you are openly disgusted with me. I know you don't think I'm attractive, and I know you think I'm fat. You can't even hide how shallow and mean you are when it comes to my looks, and whenever I try to get close to you, you grimace like you just swallowed something sour. I hate it so much, and it's so hurtful. I should just have you stuffed and keep you in my house."

I blinked several times, trying to process what he said. "I'm sorry, what?"

He laughed bitterly. "You know, have you *stuffed*. Like taxidermy. Like, say you were dead. I could get you stuffed and keep you at my house. Then I'd be able to do anything I wanted to you, and you couldn't do or say anything. And I could make sure you looked like you enjoyed it."

I was silent. How does a person even respond to something like that?

He laughed bitterly again and said, "Relax. I'm joking."

To this day, I don't know if he was. But whether his comments were meant as a joke or not, they sent me a very clear message: tread carefully. The more time I spent with him, the more I realized I only knew and saw the parts of Kip Arnold that he wanted me to see. There was more to him than I could possibly imagine, and it wasn't just unsettling; it was dangerous.

While our disturbing conversations were reserved for times when we were on the phone, thankfully, his increased presence with my flag team finally raised concerns. Not too long after he started helping out with my flag team—weeks, maybe a month later—the school received an anonymous tip that I had been seen riding in Kip Arnold's car. As I was getting ready for my next class after flag practice, I checked my phone and saw I had a voicemail. I listened to Arnold's panicked voice as he told me someone had filed a report about us. He said I was probably going to get called in to talk to school administration.

Arnold sounded frantic as he signed off with, "Get rid of the phone I gave you, and deny everything. Tell them I'm a great guy and really talk me up to them. If they ask why I'm around you so much, just say I help you with your homework and school stuff, and everything will be fine. This is all gonna blow over."

I knew I had to lie. I was absolutely terrified of what Arnold was capable of if I told the administration the truth about what he had done to me. But it wasn't just that. Juan was on campus that day, and I couldn't let him find out. Plus, there had recently been other incidents with a few other teachers and students at my high school, and I saw how harshly the other kids at my school reacted to them. The general consensus was that the girls were sluts who were asking for it, and the teachers were basically just caught up in their web. And since one of the girls was a former member of the flag team, it wasn't uncommon to hear about how slutty all of the flag girls were. I could practically hear my fellow students going after me and my character; I could sense the blame they would heap on me if the truth became public.

Ultimately, I was called out of class and brought into the dean's office, where I was met by school administrators *and* two police officers. I was terrified, but I tried to keep my cool as I sat down to talk with them. I was completely on my own—no parent, lawyer, or advocate was with me as they started with their questions. The entire room surged with hostile energy. I was certain they were making assumptions about me and just waiting to hear me confirm that I was as bad of a person as they thought. I didn't feel like these people were my saviors, extending a hand to help me out of a bad situation. They felt like accusers, ready to pounce, pushing me to admit my wrongdoings so they could call me out for being such a depraved girl.

Looking back, I can't help but wonder if that really was the energy they were trying to convey. Maybe they were just trying to get to the bottom of Arnold's behavior and truly did want to help me. Still, this was my impression because I was so blinded by the grooming and manipulation from Arnold and crippled by shame and the fear of how my family, my boyfriend, and fellow students would react. But whatever the truth, I didn't feel safe, so I lied about everything that happened between us.

The officers asked, "Has Mr. Arnold ever touched you inappropriately?"

"No."

"Did Mr. Arnold ever say anything inappropriate to you?"

"No."

"Has Mr. Arnold ever threatened you?"

"No," I said.

They ticked off behavior after behavior, all things that he definitely had done, and I denied them all. My heart pounded so hard in my chest, I was certain they had to be able to hear it. My whole body shook, and I was certain they'd see it and know every word I said was a lie. I tried my best to force a smile as I talked about what a great guy Arnold was and how much he had helped me with my schoolwork. As I spoke, my head spun with all the possible scenarios if they did decide something sketchy was happening between us. The look of betrayal in Juan's eyes. The whispers from classmates. The rumors. The loneliness. I tried to shake the images from my head, forced a bigger smile on my face, and continued to talk up Arnold.

I was in that room for a long time, as the officers would circle back and repeat questions, trying to make sure my story stayed consistent. And despite my nerves, I didn't waver. I don't know if they ultimately chose to believe me or realized I wasn't going to give anything away. Either way, they decided they had what they needed and sent me on my way.

However, the school wasn't ready to give up on the situation just yet, so they contacted my dad. They called him into the administration office to talk, and I waited in the hallway. As they left the office, I saw my father's face, and he looked completely stricken. Horrified, I watched from across the hall as he finished with the administrators, his expression becoming increasingly upset. I don't know what was said specifically, but I knew they were talking to him about Kip Arnold. After they were done talking to my dad, we headed to the car to go home. My dad seethed with anger, and we walked in tense silence. I didn't know what to think. What had they said to him? What were they going to do? What was my dad going to do? I had a brief glimmer of hope that maybe my dad was going to come to my defense and help me find my way out of the mess I was in with Arnold. But that didn't last long.

"What is happening? You're involved with the police now, Cindy?"

I turned to look at him and opened my mouth to answer, but he cut me off.

"I don't even know who you are anymore. I can't believe you're involved in something like this. What is this I'm hearing about you and a teacher? I don't know what's going on, but I know you're a bitch and a slut. I am so ashamed of you."

As we stepped closer to the car, I noticed that Arnold had shown up at the school. I watched as he struck up a conversation with an old student of his, acting as if it were a totally normal day. I was horrified. What was he *doing* there? Was he there for me? Was he there to talk to Juan? I could tell by his relaxed demeanor that he was trying to act as if nothing was wrong to convince the administration that he was a good guy, but I had no idea why he thought showing up at my school was a good idea. I also didn't know if he planned to approach me and my dad, and with how angry my father was, I was certain that interaction wouldn't end well. Thankfully, Arnold kept his distance, and I got in the car. Of course, my dad was still furious, and he continued to tell me how disgusting I was and what a disappointment and embarrassment I was for getting involved with a teacher and the police.

His ranting continued the entire way home. He didn't stop to let me respond, and he didn't bother to hear my side of the story. Instead, he spent the entire car ride hammering into me that I was a bitch, a slut, a disappointment.

When I got home, he stormed into the house, and he and my mom fought as he demanded to know what she knew about "the teacher." My mother denied any knowledge of anything and played dumb about Arnold having any place in my life. She never owned up to giving her blessing when it came to our phone conversations. They yelled as much as either of them could take, and then they stormed off in separate directions.

My mom walked up to me, her face expressionless, and said, "Your father's very upset."

Arnold and I didn't really talk after that. He did call me shortly after I got home that day to make sure I stuck to my story. Once he felt satisfied that I hadn't turned him in, he told me he was certain everything would just blow over, but we should lay low and keep our distance for now. So we did.

My junior year ended, and my senior year began with zero communication between Arnold and me. But the situation didn't just blow over as Arnold had hoped. The school district started looking more closely into Arnold and ultimately reprimanded him. However, they didn't fire him, they didn't remove him from a position where he interacted with students, and they didn't bring any formal charges against him. Instead, they reassigned him to another school meant to be a sort of rehabilitation assignment for teachers, but he was still interacting with students every day.

And while I thought I would feel so free with the break from Arnold, that period of silence was incredibly hard for me. Suddenly, I found myself all alone. My parents thought I was garbage, and they didn't ever waste time telling me. So I did everything I could to stay out of my house. Thankfully, my relationship with Juan meant that I was frequently gone on dates and to parties with his family. Even with Juan being such a refuge from my parents, there was a huge part of my life I was keeping from him. Juan had no idea what was happening with Arnold, and he hadn't even found out why the school questioned me.

When I needed to escape even further than an outing with Juan could take me, I read. The first *Twilight* movie had recently come out, and I loved the story, so I started reading the books. I began to fall in love with reading as a way to escape my reality because the truth of my situation was an ugly one, and I didn't want anyone to know. Not only did I keep Arnold a secret from Juan, but I hid Arnold from my friends so well that even my best friend had no idea anything was wrong outside of my family situation. And it was easy to focus on my problems at home, because it felt like we were constantly fighting.

My mother hated how much I was out of the house, and it started to sour her perspective on Juan. Suddenly, she nagged me about everything I was doing. Why was I reading so much instead of doing something for the family or my future? Why couldn't I just get a job? Why was I leaving the house just to read alone? Why couldn't I do something productive? Why was I spending so much time with Juan? My mother was still dragging me to church and trying to get me interested in Christianity, and I was missing church more frequently because of dates with Juan, so she started calling Juan a rock in my path.

But the criticism didn't stop there. When the weather was nice, Juan and I liked to go to the beach a lot, and I wasn't great about applying sunscreen. So it wasn't unusual for me to come home with a really dark tan or a sunburn. This drove my mother crazy. She tore into me for spending all day wasting time or spending my days with Juan, and then she started mocking me for how dark I was becoming. She commented on how ugly I looked with such dark skin and frequently pretended to gag or vomit because of how dark I was getting. She made it clear that she thought my boyfriend was trash and that I was disgusting, careless, and sinful when I spent time with him.

I was beginning to see that my family dynamic wasn't just abnormal; it was straight-up toxic. As I spent more time with Juan and his family at parties, holiday events, and family dinners, the difference between their dynamic and what I experienced at home became glaringly obvious. Juan's family wasn't perfect, and they certainly fought. However, there was an overwhelming sense that they were all in it together. They cared about their own individual lives, but they also cared about making sure the other members of the family felt loved and supported.

Juan's mother was incredibly strict and didn't suffer fools. She held everyone and everything to incredibly high standards, so it wasn't rare for her to get angry about something that someone else might say wasn't a big deal. She was nice but a firecracker. Even in the face of her random, occasional bursts of rage, she didn't discard you or tear down your worth as a human being if you messed up. She let you know you did a bad thing, but then she walked alongside you as you worked to pick up the pieces. I started to realize that not having a single person in my family I could confide in or ask for advice wasn't normal or healthy. And it wasn't standard parenting practice to teach children the right thing to do by scaring or demeaning them into submission. The realization that my parents had chosen to create such a toxic household made me want to spend even less time with my family.

Of course, my mom could feel me pulling away and she hated the choices I was making, so she kept pounding me with criticism and shame. She didn't know how disgusting I already felt, and how much self-hatred I was carrying for what Arnold had done to me, but I knew it ultimately wouldn't have mattered to her. Regardless, I couldn't talk to my family about it. Whenever situations surrounding Arnold had come up with people like my dad or during the school's investigation, it was clear that Arnold wasn't the bad guy—I was bad for letting him into my life. So the conspiracy of silence continued, as I knew I couldn't talk to my friends about Arnold if I wanted to ensure no one started spreading rumors about me. And I certainly couldn't talk to Juan about it, because I knew he would dump me as soon as I came clean about Arnold.

I was alone.

I was trash.

No one truly understood me.

I needed help, but because of the crushing weight of my secret, I couldn't ask for the help I needed. And every time I was in a situation where glimmers of truth about Arnold came out, the person who found out always reacted with shock and disgust toward me. Any time I had an opportunity to share what was really going on, I pushed people away. I didn't need anyone else to tell me how awful I was, and it was clear that no one was coming to my aid—mainly, as I believed at the time, because I didn't deserve it. I kept everyone at arm's length, and the more I realized I couldn't let Juan see the real truth about me, I started pushing him away too. Understandably, he was confused. He didn't know why I kept putting up emotional barriers between us and why I so frequently flinched or shied away from moments where he'd try to get physically intimate with me. As I dealt with all of those intense feelings of loneliness and worthlessness, I turned to the one person that I could talk to about everything. The one person who knew more about me than anyone else and who was one of the best listeners I had ever met.

After months of silence, I called Kip Arnold.

CHAPTER FIVE
RECONNECTED

Admit it: you think I'm crazy for calling Arnold. What was I thinking? Why would I consciously make contact with a man who, through years of abuse and manipulation, was destroying my life? I don't know if I can explain why I called him in a way that would make sense to someone who hasn't been in a similar situation. But that was a dark time for me, and things looked bleak; I saw my life through the warped perspective Arnold had so carefully crafted.

Added to that, my home life was toxic and my relationship with Juan was becoming tenuous. Every choice I made seemed to upset either my family or Juan. Apparently, I was constantly doing the wrong thing, and I felt more worthless as time went on. I began to wonder if I was a total waste of a person. Plus, any time someone I knew found out about Arnold—or if I saw someone that I knew go public with a situation similar to mine—the end result was an outpouring of blame and disgust for the student. I figured that the pain I felt from what happened with Arnold must be self-inflicted. So, if there really wasn't any way out of this pit I had fallen into, and if I was doomed to forever be perceived as a disappointment and a whore, I might as well turn to the one person who made me feel like I wasn't a waste of space and total trash. Someone who knew my entire story and still thought I was something special. Because somehow Arnold had managed to still be that for me.

Of course, Arnold was well aware of that fact. He used situations like this in the past to champion himself as the one source of acceptance and stability. He worked tirelessly (indirectly assisted by my parents) to distort my reality and turn everyone around me into monsters who could never understand or appreciate me like he did. While he couldn't have predicted the investigation at my school, his aim from the beginning had been to foster an intense need and reliance in me for his validation and acceptance. He had groomed and manipulated me to believe there was no one else who would ever accept me. So, when a need arose for a season of prolonged distance between us, he knew without a doubt that I couldn't share my story with anyone but him.

And that's exactly what happened. Arnold was able to expertly wedge himself further into my life. He comforted me, promised that my parents were wrong about me, and reassured me that my own thoughts of self-doubt were wrong. I was just a silly, young girl who didn't know what she wanted or needed in life. But as the older, wiser adult who cared deeply about me, he assured that he could help me achieve the life I always dreamed of—that he would always be there to show me what I wanted, what I needed, and give those things to me. He swore he loved me and could take care of me. He promised me everything would be okay.

But first I had to dump Juan immediately—or else.

"I'm a very vengeful person, Cindy," he warned me. "I don't think you want to keep playing with me like this. You need to realize what you're doing and who you're messing with. It's about time you got rid of that kid."

That phone call was like a spark that erupted into an inferno as he burst back into my life. He started ramping up his stalking behaviors, and I knew I couldn't go anywhere without him close behind. He followed me, he followed Juan, he would park outside of my house or my school, and he made sure that everywhere I turned, I saw him. By fanning the flame with that one phone call, I had inadvertently given him a renewed sense of energy that he poured into reminding me that I wouldn't ever be able to get away from him.

He called and texted me at all hours of the day. My phone was constantly buzzing, so I did my best to keep it on silent so Juan wouldn't notice. Although I knew better than to save Arnold's number in my phone, there were a few times when Juan noticed the same number calling several times, and told me I should just answer the phone to see who was calling.

One time, I actually did it.

I feigned confusion over who was calling. "Hello?"

"Are you with Chunti?"

I cleared my throat and looked at Juan. I knew he couldn't hear Arnold's end of the conversation, so I sighed and said yes.

"Put me on speaker."

"What?"

"Put me on speaker. I want to talk to him."

"I don't think that's a good idea."

"Nah! Do it, Cindy! I want to talk to the kid who's taking up so much of your time and causing me so much heartbreak. Do it. *Put me on speaker.*"

I realized it would probably raise more questions from Juan if I just suddenly hung up, so I did it. My pulse was racing as I tried to think of what he might say as I switched the call to speaker.

"Hey! Juan, are you there?" Arnold asked.

Juan smiled and furrowed his brow in confusion, pointing to the phone and mouthing, *Who is this?*

I mouthed the first thing I could think of: *Cousin.*

Juan nodded. "Hey! Yeah, I'm here!"

Arnold laughed. "Nice to finally talk to you. I've heard a lot about you. A lot."

My stomach dropped.

Juan chuckled. "I hope it's all good stuff!"

Arnold barked out a sinister-sounding laugh, and my eyes darted nervously to Juan. Had he noticed the edge to Arnold's laugh? I needed to put a stop to this. *Now.* I could feel Arnold circling in on Juan to attack and reveal the truth. So I quickly burst out in a fake giggle to distract them.

"Anyway! You've officially met Juan! We're trying to hang out, so I'll talk to you later, okay? Bye!"

"Hey, wait, I—" Arnold shouted quickly as I hung up the phone.

I drew a deep breath and smiled at Juan. Not wanting to field any more questions about this new "cousin" for fear that Juan would start wondering how this very white-sounding man was a member of my Salvadoran family, I quickly rolled my eyes and shrugged, "Family, right? They're crazy!"

Juan laughed and nodded; he didn't seem too fazed by it.

From then on, I tried to be extra certain that my phone didn't go off too much when I was with Juan. In addition to silencing it, I often left it at home (telling Arnold it needed to charge—even if it had full battery) or turned it off completely (telling Arnold it had died). But that didn't stop Arnold from finding new ways to pester me. He started an online account with my cell phone provider so he was able to see all of my incoming and outgoing calls and frequently asked me about who I was talking to. He also got a burner phone so he could call me using a number he hoped I wouldn't recognize.

Arnold was everywhere, constantly nagging me to dump Juan, checking up on me, and identifying new ways to worm his way into my life. It was my senior year—what was supposed to be the most fun part of high school—and I was drowning. I was never a straight A student, but I usually brought home As and Bs. I loved my English class and writing, but the stress caused my grades to dip, even in the classes I loved. Arnold consistently coached me on ways I could improve at school, as he knew I wanted to attend college at UCLA or Cal State Long Beach, but my grades kept sliding. I began taking an acting class, and just when I was starting to really enjoy it, Arnold ruined that aspect of my life as well. At every audition I attended, the answer was the same: We like you, but we need some headshots. Headshots were expensive, and I just didn't have the money to afford them. Arnold knew that, and he knew my parents couldn't afford them either, so he offered time and again to pay for them. He finally offered to serve as my manager and that was the last straw. I abandoned my acting aspirations.

During this time, I continued pushing Juan away, which only aggravated the tension between us. At home, life with my parents had become more toxic than ever. Plus, my mother had started to notice Arnold occasionally waiting outside of her house. Her hatred of Juan growing every day, she would yell at me for treating Arnold so poorly. In her mind, Arnold wasn't stalking me. I was standing him up for Juan—a boy who wasn't rich, pulled me away from my home and activities that my mom approved of, and clearly couldn't care for me like she believed Arnold could. In her mind, I was standing up and manipulating a nice rich man to spend time with a boy she thought was a piece of trash and a rock in my path.

She also wasn't shy about reminding me that I was trash and deserved the blame for anything bad that happened to me. For example, one day I was wearing a Juicy Couture necklace as I walked home from school with my best friend Leah. We noticed a sketchy-looking man near us, and we scooted away from him to give him some space to pass us. Suddenly, the man ran up to me without saying a word and reached for me. He grabbed at my necklace, tugging on it with all of his might until he was able to yank it off my neck, and ran off. Furious, Leah raced after the man. Despite my shouts for her to come back and leave him alone, she chased after him until he hopped in his car and drove off. We raced back to my house, hearts pounding. Once we got to the front of my family's apartment and were sure we were safe, Leah gave me a quick hug, promised to check in on me later, and started toward her house. My brother-in-law was the only one home at the time and startled at the sound of me bursting inside.

"What is going on?!" he shouted.

"I just got robbed!" I sobbed. "We were walking home from school, not doing anything, and this random man ran up to me, grabbed at my neck, and yanked at my necklace. He pulled it right off and got away! Look at my neck! Leah said it's all red and scratched up from his nasty fingers. She said she thought she saw a bruise starting to form too!"

I looked at my brother-in-law, expecting him to ask me some sort of follow-up questions or check to see if I was okay. Instead, he just nodded, made a "yikes" face, and turned back to whatever he had been doing. With my heart still pounding and tears streaming down my face, I sighed at his indifference and walked to the bathroom to check out my neck and try to calm down, all alone.

When my mother came home from work, I told her what happened. To my shock and frustration, she not only didn't care about what happened, but she started blaming *me*.

"I don't know why you're so upset, and you'd better not bother the police about this. I can't believe you thought it was a good idea to wear something like that out! You should have known wearing flashy jewelry would invite attention. You were asking for someone to try and take it from you. Next time, don't make such foolish choices."

I struggled to process the depths of my mother's cruelty. I hadn't expected her to be as upset as I was, but I at least thought she would show some maternal concern for my injured neck. She didn't. I had just been robbed, and it was my fault. I felt so alone in that moment. My poor choices had invited the robber's attack, and if I had been smarter or hadn't been so interested in being noticed and looking good, that robber wouldn't have clocked me.

Not long after, Leah's mother called me to check up on me. I could hear the concern in her voice the second we started talking, and it made me feel a little better. Leah's mom was always great at filling that nurturing motherly role for me.

"Cindy! How are you doing? Leah told me what happened! Are you okay?"

I said yes, but I could hear my voice wavering as a new round of sobs started inching their way up my throat. Something about the mixture of sadness and fear paired with the tender way Leah's mom spoke to me turned me into a blubbering mess.

"Oh, *mija*," she said, "I'm so sorry this happened to you. You must have been so scared! How's your neck?"

I sniffled. "It's okay. There's definitely a bruise and some scratches, but it'll be okay."

"Did you tell your mom?"

"Yes," I said weakly.

"And what did she say?"

I sniffed again as I tried to keep some composure on the phone. "She said I shouldn't be wearing such flashy jewelry."

Leah's mom cleared her throat, and the line was silent for a moment. I could tell that she was as shocked at my mom's reaction as I was and was trying to figure out how to respond.

She cleared her throat one more time and said, "I'm going to come check on you later, okay? Hang in there, *mija*." I smiled weakly and hung up the phone.

Juan was working, but I wanted him to know what had happened. So I called and told him the whole story, including my mom's reaction, trying my best to keep my tears at bay.

"Wait. So, are you okay?!" he asked with a panicked edge to his voice.

"I've got a few scratches and bruises, but I'm okay."

He sighed, "I told you not to be walking so late at night!"

"Juan! Are you kidding me? That's not what I need to hear right now! I just got robbed, my mom's blaming me for what happened, and I don't need that from you too! I was just walking home, and I wasn't even alone!"

He sighed again. "I know; you're right. I'm sorry. I just get so worried about you. I don't want anything to happen to you. Are you going to be okay?"

"Yeah. I'm just freaked out."

"Okay. Well, I'm still worried about you. I'm gonna leave work early, and I'll come check on you. I think you need to make a police report. If you want, I can help you do it when I come over. I don't care what your mom says—this is a big deal, and you need to say something."

I agreed to make a police report, we hung up, and I tried to relax. Not long after, Leah's mom showed up to check on me and talk with my mother.

I let her in, and she gave me a hug and started investigating my neck. My mother was in the kitchen and essentially ignored us the entire time.

"You poor thing! Look at that bruise! I can't believe that happened to you!" She gave me a hug, shot a stern glance into the kitchen toward my mother, and then looked back at me, "Have you been able to calm down at all?"

I nodded. "Yeah, I think I'll feel even better after I get some rest."

She smiled and gave me another hug, and then looked into the kitchen again. My mother was still ignoring us, so Leah's mother walked over to her.

"Can you believe what happened to Cindy?"

My mom rolled her eyes. "She was robbed in Los Angeles. What a shock!" she said, her voice dripping with sarcasm.

Leah's mom balked. "I would think it's always a shock to hear your daughter was robbed, regardless of where you live."

My mother waved her off. "She should have known better. Wearing such flashy jewelry, Cindy was asking for someone to rob her—or worse. She knows it, too."

Leah's mother and my mom went back and forth a bit like that, my mother refusing to admit that something bad had happened to me. I could see Leah's mother getting heated. She opened her mouth, clearly about to let a big insult fly, then shut it quickly.

"I can see we just aren't going to agree here," Leah's mom said curtly. "I suppose I'll just leave you alone then."

My mother nodded and returned to her work in the kitchen. Leah's mom turned to me, gave me another hug, and whispered in my ear, "I'm so sorry this happened to you."

I smiled, walked her out, and went to my room. Leah's mother had always been very kind to me, and at that point, I was well aware that my family dynamic was abnormal. But I still wanted to give my mom the benefit of the doubt. After all, she was my mother. Surely, she had to know best, right? Surely, she had to know more about me and my life than a friend's mom—even a close friend's mom. Right?

At Juan's insistence, I filed a police report when he stopped by after work, but the police weren't able to do much. I couldn't help but internalize my mother's reaction to all areas of my life. My actions were the cause for the bad things that happened to me; it was all my fault. Naturally, that idea seeped into Arnold's place in my life.

I couldn't get rid of him, and I was starting to fear that I had dug myself into a bottomless pit. Maybe he'd never leave—he certainly wasn't letting up in how frequently he called me and wanted to spend time with me. And the more Arnold tried to force his way into my life, the more confusing his intentions became. One day he said he was just trying to be a good friend and listened while I poured my heart out about the latest fight I had with my mom. Or he gave me advice on school drama or stress I experienced from a class I wasn't doing well in. Then the next day, he flipped entirely and only wanted to talk about sexual things. He reminded me of his "joke" about how he should have me stuffed so he could do whatever he wanted to me whenever he wanted. I never knew where I stood with him, I never knew what to expect, and I couldn't escape. He was constantly there—calling, texting, showing up at flag practice—trying to wedge his way into my life however he could.

It was exhausting. Anytime I began to consider a way out, he reminded me what a vengeful person he was, shared about the latest way he managed to follow Juan without Juan noticing, or commented about having me stuffed. There was so much noise in my life and within my own head and heart that I frequently ventured into the auditorium at school and just sat at the back in the dark. I let the darkness surround me until the silence grew so loud that it would make my ears ring and provide some respite—some peace. I never left with any sudden clarity but that moment away from the cacophony and chaos of my life gave me a little extra strength to keep pushing forward.

When prom rolled around, Arnold began bugging me about letting him buy me a new prom dress.

"I don't want you to buy me another dress. I can figure it out on my own. And if nothing else, I can wear the dress from last year."

"See, you just don't understand anything. You can't do something like that. You want to keep Juan interested, right? Besides, it's your senior prom. This is a big deal. Let me do this for you. I know what's best for you, and I just want you to have a nice prom."

I was silent for a moment. As usual I didn't know what to think. I couldn't help but remember how our prom dress shopping trip had ended last year. But at the same time, a lot had happened since then, and he was even more unpredictable. His moods changed so rapidly, and I wasn't sure he even realized why I might have negative memories about prom dress shopping with him.

"I don't think so."

"Oh, come on, Cindy! You can't ask your parents for money. And you don't know how to drive. If you're magically able to find some cash, how are you even going to get to the store? You need me, and you know it. And you're not about to burden your parents with this. They're worried enough about your grades. Do you really think it's an okay thing to ask them for money when you think you might not even walk at graduation? You know that's messed up."

"Listen, I've—"

"I'm not taking no for an answer on this, Cindy. I'll keep asking. Just let me do this. You know I'll get you a dress that's nicer than anything you could get for yourself. You wouldn't even know where to start looking."

After days and days of calls like this, he had worn me down to the point that I finally agreed. He had been on a nice streak, so I was starting to feel safe with him again. Plus, it wasn't the first time he had shopped for me since last year's prom. He was constantly buying me designer purses, shoes, and jewelry—even though I never asked for anything. So it wasn't a surprise when he suggested dress shopping. But just like the previous prom, he didn't take my opinion into account. He knew he couldn't go with me to prom and that I would be going with Juan. However, if I went with Juan, then Arnold had to be certain there was a physical reminder that he was still in my life—a visible way he was able to exert his influence over me in that moment.

I tried on every dress he suggested, and whenever I offered my thoughts, he waved his hand dismissively and shook his head. "No, you don't understand what looks good and what guys like to see. You're too immature to understand this stuff, Cindy." And with that, he directed me to another dress he liked. When he landed on a dress that was his favorite, he bought it for me, despite my insistence that I could pay for it myself.

As we drove home, I realized we weren't heading toward my house.

"Where are we going?"

"Sorry, I just remembered I forgot to feed my dog. She's gonna lose it if she doesn't get her lunch. I'm just gonna give her some food, and we can go."

I shrugged and nodded. As I walked onto his boat, I saw his dog and turned to Arnold, expecting him to open a can of dog food. Instead, I saw that intense predatory look in his eyes as he headed toward me.

"I have waited long enough. You're eighteen now. I'm going to take what's mine."

My blood ran cold as I instinctively took a few steps backward. I was mentally screaming at myself, furious that I had walked into another trap. My heart pounded and my entire body quaked. My mom's words after the robbery reverberated in my brain. What had I been thinking going shopping with Arnold? I had been too concerned about looking nice at the prom and too worried about keeping Arnold on the hook. Of course, he wanted something from me. It was my fault for being too shallow to see through the ruse, and my poor choices had led me right back to his boat.

I could feel the nausea rise like a tidal wave from the pit of my stomach. My body felt like it was on fire, and every time he tried to reach out and touch me, it was like needles stabbing my skin. I was so scared and so angry with myself. But once again, I realized I was completely helpless. No one was looking for me. No one would hear me if I screamed. My own parents had labeled me as a disgusting slut, so I was certain there wasn't a soul on Earth who would be interested in coming to my rescue. Besides, I had turned eighteen the September of my senior year. It had been several months since then, so I was an undisputed legal adult, and I was sure this probably wouldn't even be considered rape. I know now that it was most certainly rape, but at the time I was convinced I was just asking for it, yet again. I had sunk lower than ever before, and the only way out was to get through this attack.

Still, I tried to tell him no. I tried to push him away when he shoved me onto the tiny couch, but he didn't listen. It was hopeless. As he thrust his weight on top of me, I lay there, lifeless, like a rag doll. It was the first time he raped me vaginally. And unlike the time in his hotel room when

I was in middle school, he didn't have trouble penetrating me. As brutally and ruthlessly as before, he pounded against my body. Tears streamed down my face, but Arnold didn't care. When he was finished, he started screaming at me.

"You're not a virgin! I can tell! You're not a virgin! You've had sex with Chunti, haven't you?"

I didn't answer. I couldn't move. I couldn't look at him. I couldn't think.

"I can't believe you did this! I've been faithful, you whore! You're a slut and a liar! Get off my boat, you piece of trash!"

Expressionless and emotionless, I dressed and started to leave. He was right. I wasn't a virgin. Juan and I had had sex. I guess I really was a cheater, a liar, and a whore like he said. *Garbage.* Look what I kept letting him do to me. Look how I kept lying to Juan. How could anyone love someone like me?

Arnold drove me home, screaming at me the entire time. I remained silent, looking out the window, tears coursing down my face. The shame was unbearable. I absorbed all of the insults he hurled at me, internalizing every single word. He told me I was worthless, that I was a whore, that I was evil, manipulative, a cheater. And I believed him. Here I was, having just been raped by this monster, and I felt like I had somehow done something wrong or deserved it in some way. Because, at the very least, I wasn't telling the truth. I was having sex with Juan while I continued to talk with Arnold. That was something a slut did, right? So that's what I had to be.

It would have been nice if I had felt safe to talk to my mother about what had happened, but I was delusional if I thought that conversation would end well. I couldn't bear to have so much shame heaped on me from another person, so I continued to suffer in silence. I felt more alone than ever. Each day I felt worse about myself because Arnold would call me regularly just to yell at me—and I picked up every time. The very least I could do was let him get his feelings off his chest, right?

But I couldn't tell Juan the truth about what I was fighting with. Even if I did manage to get Arnold out of my life for good, what exactly would I have left? Who would I have who was truly in my corner? Who would I have who would care about my thoughts, my dreams, and the deepest truths about my struggles? I hated to admit it, but because of how closely I guarded my secret about Arnold's abuse, no one else in my life knew me as well as Arnold did. I had friends, but I kept them at arm's length to hide the parts of myself I was most ashamed of. And no one in my family was remotely interested in hearing about any of my deeper issues, especially something like this. Juan was there, but once he found out about Arnold, I was certain he'd feel so betrayed that I'd never see him again. I truly had no one outside of Kip Arnold.

My life prospects weren't much better either. My grades were bad and getting worse every day. I had no idea what I wanted to do with my life. I had no job, no money, and no family connections that could get me plugged into an industry to jumpstart my career. The cold reality was starting to set in that my best prospect might actually be spending the rest of my life with Kip Arnold on his horrible boat.

Hopelessness, sadness, and depression settled on me like a heavy blanket. Every day, I felt like I was trying to walk through thick fog and sticky mud at the same time. I couldn't see clearly, and any attempt to move forward or make a decision exhausted me. I didn't know how I was supposed to find my way out on my own, and the longer I fought it, the more I started to fear that I had just gotten myself into too big of a mess. Sometimes things are too broken or too dirty to fix, and I was beginning to feel like I was one of those things. I was too tired to call for help, but even if I did have the energy, I knew there wasn't anyone I could reach out to. Once people heard my story, I was certain no one would want to help me. The realization was heartbreaking, but it got me thinking: Was I even someone worth saving anymore? As I looked at how the people around me treated one another, and without any sort of relationship with Jesus or any faith or belief in a higher power to lean on, it seemed I really might be too far gone.

Arnold had sucked the life out of me. All that was left was an empty shell. Still, I didn't place all of the blame on him. Yes, I hated what he had done to me, but I was certain my actions put me in those scenarios. I had chosen poorly; I had led him on; and I had created this hellish life for myself where I had absolutely no one and no future prospects, except to spend the rest of my life in a shitty boat with the man who had been grooming, manipulating, assaulting, and raping me since I was fourteen. I told myself I had *let* him attack me. I kept thinking about myself in such hateful ways, using the names I'd been called since I was a child innocently trying on a spaghetti strap shirt. *Disgusting. Slut. Stupid. Horrible. Worthless.* My depression weighed me down so much that everything started to feel too exhausting and painful. Listening to people talk. Speaking. Walking. Thinking. Moving. It was all too much. I just wanted to be still. I didn't want to be around anyone. I didn't want to be touched. I just wanted quiet and peace. I wanted to be left alone.

Almost immediately after the second rape on his boat, I realized that what I really wanted was to not be alive anymore. I hated myself, and I was disgusted with myself, down to my very core. There was no saving me, and I wasn't worth saving anyway. I was lying to Juan, unfairly putting him in a situation he had never asked for. And as Arnold's stalking behavior ramped up once again, I feared I was putting Juan in constant danger too. Who knew what Arnold would do if he was able to get a moment alone with Juan. And even though I hated Arnold, I still felt guilty, like I was leading him on or playing with his emotions. I was pretty sure my mom's assumptions about his bank account were way off, but I also felt like a terrible daughter for not being willing to consider him as an option if it meant providing her with a happier and more stable life. I was hurting the man I loved, I was hurting another man, and I was neglecting my mom's needs. My internal moral compass was clearly broken. With every passing day, it became clearer that the world would be far better off without me in it.

One day, standing in my bathroom, I glanced at my razor. I thought, *I could slash my wrists and it would be over.* I reached for the razor and stopped short. *There's no way I'd have the guts to cut myself deep enough. Though, I guess I don't even know how deep you're supposed to cut. Is my razor even sharp enough to do that? What if I just end up needing stiches and just leave myself in a ton of pain and make a huge, awful mess for my parents to clean up?* I looked at the medicine cabinet. *I could swallow every pill in the house. I'd probably just go to sleep and never wake up. It wouldn't even hurt.* I liked that idea. No pain. Just sleep. Peace. Finally. But another thought nagged me. *What kind of medication do I think my parents have, exactly? We don't have a lot of prescriptions around here. How much Tylenol do you have to take to fatally overdose? I'd probably just end up puking my brains out and needing to get my stomach pumped. Big pain, big mess, zero results.* Then I remembered my father had a gun for his job as a security guard. *I could shoot myself in the head. Bang. Done.* But the image of me shooting myself made my blood run cold. *What if Dad caught me getting his gun? Or worse yet, what if I don't die when I shoot myself? I could be left with intense brain damage from the bullet. I could be completely immobile or nonverbal for the rest of my life and have to rely on others for everything forever.*

I threw up my hands in frustration. It always seemed so easy for people to decide to end their lives in the movies. Why was I having such a hard time? Why couldn't I just make a plan and stick to it? I thought about the options I had laid out for myself, and a few other suicide methods zipped through my head, but none of them seemed like a good idea. The more I thought about it, the more I realized I wasn't afraid of dying. I wasn't even really afraid of the pain. I was afraid of surviving. That was the thought that kept me poking holes in every plan—every option I came up with had a chance of survival. I couldn't think of anything more horrific than trying to kill myself and failing. My parents would be furious. They'd maybe have me committed to a psychiatric hospital on an involuntary hold. Maybe they'd kick me out. At the very least they'd rake me over the coals for doing something so stupid and selfish, especially if my attempt left a physical mess as well as a psychological one.

But worst of all, I thought about the ways Arnold could use a suicide attempt as the ultimate tool for manipulation. That would be his opportunity to tell Juan everything. Maybe he'd even try to convince Juan that I tried to kill myself because of him, not Arnold. Maybe he'd use the attempted suicide as another way to worm his way closer into my life. And if I had any sort of injury or disability after a failed attempt, I'm sure my mom would be grateful to hand me over to him so she wouldn't have to worry about caring for me.

I leaned against the wall and slid down to the floor and let the tears silently fall. There wasn't a way out of this—not even death. I was truly trapped. I didn't want to live anymore; I knew that for certain. I just wanted to go to sleep and never wake up, but barring some sort of miracle, I knew that wouldn't happen.

So I kept on living as much as I could with such a deep level of hopelessness. I was trapped in this endless cycle with Arnold. I was trapped from ever truly opening up to Juan, having the free and honest relationship I wanted. I was trapped living out this life until something finally came along to kill me. There was no way out of my connections with Arnold, no way out of living. I would just have to keep trudging through the fog and mud for the rest of my life and hope that I was able to figure out some way to keep Juan in my life—and make him not hate me when the truth about Arnold inevitably came to light.

Juan had sensed something was off for a while, and he could tell I distanced myself more every day. When we tried to be intimate, I flinched or pulled away. I was moody and erratic. He could feel me pushing him away, literally and figuratively, and he didn't understand. It hurt him and made him angry. I hated how much pain I caused him, but I couldn't help how I acted. I felt like I was being ripped apart. I loved Juan and wanted to be with him, but my dark secret was eating me alive. I hated that I couldn't get Arnold out of my life, and I hated keeping something so huge from Juan.

More than anything, I just wanted to live a normal life and have a normal relationship with the man I was falling deeper and deeper in love with. But with the huge shadow of Kip Arnold looming over us, I feared that we could never truly have a full, happy life together. Because I knew Juan would eventually find out what was happening—either Arnold would tell him, Juan would piece it together on his own, or I'd finally break down and tell him everything. And I had no idea how he would react when he found out. Juan was fun, loving, and cared for me, but if my father's reaction to Kip Arnold's place in my life was any measure, I couldn't imagine a world where Juan would understand and forgive me, and I didn't really blame him.

At the same time, at home, my parents and my sister kept to themselves, so no one seemed to notice that anything was wrong. Or, if they did, they didn't care. My mother kept pushing me to leave Juan and get serious with Arnold.

"Juan is trash," she said. "Don't make a stupid choice and be with him. Kip Arnold can take care of you, and he can take care of me. If you would just stop being so selfish, you'd see that he's the better choice for you."

I tried to tell her that I loved Juan, and I didn't like being with Arnold. Every time I searched for the words to explain to her why I wanted Arnold out of my life, she shut me down. Same old story: I was stupid. I was selfish. I was a slut. I was immature. I never got the chance to tell her that I didn't think Arnold was nearly as rich as she thought. She just wanted me to be quiet and do what she said. In her mind, I was clearly not seeing straight and was too emotional and childish to understand what needed to be done.

I broke up with Juan twice because of it all—partly because I just couldn't handle the pressure of the relationship with Arnold on the scene and felt staying with Juan was unfair to him, but mainly because I knew it would convince Arnold to stop bothering me. And I thought that maybe I'd be okay with a broken heart if Arnold just let up for a bit. Of course, I soon realized I loved Juan too much, and I wasn't ready to throw in the towel just yet. Both breakups were short—only a few days. Neither of us could stand being apart, but I didn't know how I could keep Juan in my life when I couldn't get Arnold to leave me alone. I also knew that I couldn't bear to lose Juan forever.

All the while, Arnold tried to show me that he could be a good boyfriend whether Juan and I were together or not. Since I was eighteen, he wasn't as scared to be seen in public with me. So he would try to take me on dates. At one point, he took me to a remote park for a sort of picnic date. Of course, our "dates" at the park only really managed to show me he had a laundry list of places he could take me where no one would notice us, and he could do whatever he wanted to me there. Even though we were technically in public at this park, it was a sprawling space where he wasn't worried about anyone seeing us.

You could often see the interstate from the places he parked his SUV, and while you might theoretically be able to see into the park from the interstate, the cars passing were basically on another planet. If a car zipped by on the interstate, it wasn't like someone could see if Arnold was hurting or assaulting me and quickly stop to save me. It was so frustrating to be so close to other people who might be able to help, or at least get him to leave me alone, yet know that the chances of that happening were virtually nonexistent. So we drove to the big park, and as soon as he found a good spot for us to hang out, we walked around a bit until he found a tree with a branch where I could sit. And while I was on the tree branch, he started humping me. His would also occasionally bring his laptop and would pull it out and start playing pornography for me in an attempt to get me aroused and interested in touching him or having sex with him.

But it did the exact opposite for me. I thought it was so gross, such a reminder to me that he had zero thought about what I wanted or my comfort level. All he cared about were his own desires, his own lustful urges. Since I was technically a legal adult, he was getting more brazen when it came to taking what he believed was his. And this park was the perfect spot for him to do that. It terrified me that he chose this giant park where you could find a secluded spot and never see another person the entire time. Just like the times he had lured me onto his boat, I felt like I was completely alone.

All of it—the attacks on his boat, in his car, the hotel, and the park, and his casual threats of having me stuffed—made his message blindingly clear: *I can be good to you, and if you're not up for it, I will be your worst nightmare, and no one will ever know or care about what happened to you.*

CHAPTER SIX
INDEBTED

My life was falling apart. My grades had tanked because I was completely unable to focus. The only time I could think at all was when I sat in the dark auditorium, so studying and homework had become virtually impossible. It became so bad that I thought I might not get to walk at graduation. My mother couldn't bear the thought, and she made sure to tell me that if I didn't walk, I'd not only be embarrassing her, but she'd be eternally disappointed in me.

She said, "I don't care what you do but you need to walk across that stage on graduation. Don't make me look like a fool, Cindy!"

My future looked bleak. I still very much wanted to die, but I had officially shelved the idea of attempting to kill myself because I couldn't figure out a fail-safe way. Instead, I walked through life in a suffocating, impenetrable fog, wishing a hole would open beneath me and the earth would swallow me up. Trying to push through and build some sort of a life while also carrying the weight of the secret of Arnold's place in my life—along with the shame, the self-doubt, and the bone-chilling fear that came with it—made it impossible to focus on anything, especially school.

Needless to say, I wasn't shocked to learn that I wouldn't get to walk at graduation. But my mother was horrified. She told me I was stupid and worthless, a disappointment who wouldn't amount to anything. I believed her. Looking at the wreckage of my life smoking around me, I didn't see anything to look forward to. When I poured my heart out to Arnold, he was always quick to tell me that my mom was wrong. Not only that, but he also told me I was very smart and even started looking into colleges for me. He learned that without a high school diploma, I would still be able to attend my local community college, so I enrolled for the fall semester. Arnold told me he saw great things for my future and even greater things—if I just let him in fully. He tried to prove how helpful and supportive he could be by filing for my financial aid, picking my class schedule, and even moving into a house close to the college campus.

Arnold continued to pressure me to dump Juan, making every effort to keep control of my life. He not only called me incessantly, but he also kept me on the phone for hours to ensure I either wasn't presently with Juan or couldn't leave to be with him. Some nights, I spent hours on the phone as we "watched a movie together," me at my house and Arnold at his new place. Arnold knew I had a strict curfew, so once he figured it was too late for me to go out to meet Juan, he finally let me hang up.

Meanwhile, Juan was completely unaware of the chokehold Arnold had on my life. He just knew something big was standing between us, but he couldn't figure out what it was. And even though I wanted nothing more than to cling more tightly to him than ever, I pushed him away because of the pain, confusion, and fear clouding my entire life. With all the noise in my life from my parents, Arnold, the pressures of school, and my own internal strife, sometimes I even ignored Juan's calls. It wasn't because I didn't want to be with him or talk to him; I just desperately needed peace and quiet. Everything felt out of control, and with Arnold investigating colleges for me, I was feeling more and more hopeless. In addition to my few brief breakups with Juan, I started to talk with other guys, too.

I no longer thought I was just damaged goods; I looked at myself like I was radioactive. Everything I touched got damaged. I wreaked havoc, caused pain, and generally ruined people's lives. Even though I felt so angry and betrayed by Arnold, I still felt wildly guilty for "cheating" on him with Juan. And even though Arnold terrified me, and I wanted to get as far away from him as possible, I couldn't help but feel like I was being shallow, silly, and flighty by not committing fully to Arnold when both he and my mother constantly told me how good he was for me. My gut was telling me to run, but their messages said I was wrong for thinking that. Why couldn't I just feel happy with Arnold? He had provided a shoulder to cry on since I first met him at fourteen. He didn't seem to care about my wishes and forced himself on me on several occasions, but maybe if I could just ignore my wild instincts and go with the flow, I'd enjoy being with him more. Right?

My mind was a mess though. I truly didn't know what to think and that relentless conflict was too much for me. I was broken. I was angry. And I was so sick of this man destroying everything in my life. I decided I wanted him gone. I didn't just stick to talking with more guys; I became incredibly hostile with Arnold. The hostility gradually built from the experience on the boat during my senior year, growing exponentially as I entered college. Arnold called frequently and stayed on the line with me for extended periods of time, but we had totally turned a corner. Gone were the days of our sweet, caring conversations. Now, we just yelled and cussed each other out. Up to that point, I had never really called him by his name or any sort of a nickname, but I suddenly found the perfect nickname for him: Douchebag. Honestly, I used it so much that you might expect that his driver's license read *Kip Douchebag Arnold*. But I didn't care if I hurt him anymore, because I was finally beginning to understand that he clearly didn't care if I was hurt. Maybe I couldn't figure out how to get him out of my life, but I wanted to make sure he knew how much I hated him.

And that freaked him out. Not only was I openly hostile toward Arnold, but he also knew I wasn't only talking with Juan anymore. He didn't know details about the guys I was talking to or if it was more serious than phone conversations—it wasn't, but he didn't need to know that. Learning that he wasn't just competing against Juan but a bunch of other faceless dudes too sent Arnold into hysterics. I wasn't fourteen anymore. The years of gaslighting, grooming, manipulation, and misinformation certainly *did* mean that he was able to control me unlike anyone else. However, I had lived a lot of life since the day we met. And the warped lens through which he made me see the world was starting to crack. I realized the world was a lot bigger than Kip Arnold.

The more I lashed out at him, the more terrified he became.

He kicked up all of his controlling behaviors. If I dropped or switched a class in college, he called to yell at me and switched the class back to whatever he originally registered for me. If I didn't answer his calls, he redialed until I picked up. If I didn't answer, he went to my house to check on what I was doing and to see whether I was with Juan or someone else. He stalked Juan when he was alone, he stalked us when we went on dates, and he called me every single day to talk for hours. While he still occasionally offered to listen if I needed to get something off my chest, he focused on his main demand: dump Juan. The number of times he called or texted me increased tenfold. Missed calls and unread texts from Arnold were the norm, and they all bore a similar message: "Dump Juan immediately, or I'm telling him everything." I had to turn off my phone sometimes for a break from the incessant buzzing.

Finally, I had a moment of clarity one night. After years and years of abuse, gaslighting, fear, and manipulation, I had enough. The only way this was ever going to stop was if I did something. For a brief, shining moment I believed I did have some power over my life. I could either acquiesce to Arnold's demands—dump Juan, marry Arnold, and live the rest of my life as his wife—or I could keep up this weird double life until everything blew up in my face. Neither option was okay with me, so I realized I needed to forge my own third option. Or, at the very least, I had to try. I had to try to fight for the life I wanted, didn't I?

Feeling brave from my realization, I confronted Arnold the next time he started berating me to dump Juan. Our calls had reached new heights of hostility, and I knew Arnold was starting to panic as he searched for new ways to control me. But I was done with fighting and staying silent and telling him what he wanted to hear in hopes of getting a few moments of peace.

"So, have you dumped Chunti yet?" he demanded for what was probably the millionth time.

"Don't call him that. And no. I'm not going to dump him. So you can just stop asking me."

"Cindy, why are you being like this? I just want to love you. I want to take care of you. He's just going to knock you up and run off, and you're going to try to come crawling back to me. And let me tell you, I don't know what I'll do when that happens. And you *know* it will. He's trash. And if you're not going to do the right thing, I'm going to tell him. Who's going to want a slut like you?"

"Shut up, douchebag. I said I'm not dumping him. So you can stop texting me and calling me about it. It isn't going to happen. And that's the end of it. You can do whatever you want because I'm done with this."

The line went quiet for a moment, and he sighed.

"If that's what you want."

I couldn't help but feel a little guilty at that reaction. I could hear the pain in his voice, and I started to doubt if I was making an even worse, crueler move than anything before. But his moment of tenderness, however feigned it likely was, was gone and instantly replaced with rage.

"Listen, you want out, all you had to do was say so. You're not going to dump Chunti, fine. But if we're through, then you need to pay me back for all the stuff I've bought you over the years."

"What are you talking about? I never asked you to buy anything. I don't owe you anything and you know it."

"Don't be stupid. Maybe you never explicitly asked for anything, but I had to throw out a lot of cash to keep you interested. I can't keep a shallow girl like you interested with a body like mine, so I had to shell out the big bucks. The clothes, the jewelry, the purses, that stuff adds up, you know. And I've spent a lot on you, so if you're going to throw that all back in my face, the least you can do is settle your tab."

"Screw you! I don't owe you *anything*, douche. I never asked for a cent; you just bought me stuff because you wanted to. I didn't want it then and I don't want it now, so I'll just give it all back."

"What the hell am I going to do with stuff like a designer purse and prom dresses, Cindy? I can't pay rent with that. You've got to pay me back in cash."

"That's crazy."

"You might think so, but if you're going to screw me over like this, I'm going to get what's mine. So you've got to pay me back for everything: the food, the gifts, my *time*, or I'll tell Juan, your family, everyone all about us."

My heart was pounding, my resolve weakening. But I could still sort of see the light at the end of the tunnel, so I relented. "Fine. How much do you think I owe you?"

"Six thousand dollars."

My jaw fell open. *Six thousand dollars?* How in the world did he think I was going to pay him six thousand dollars? He knew I didn't have a job. He knew I wasn't rich. My family wasn't rich. Juan wasn't rich. Did he think I just had six grand lying around?

But before I could grill him on how he had come to such a crazy number, I decided to just agree. He was notorious for asking me to do things, say things, or agree to things and usually I could get him to chill out if I just agreed. So I figured it would be the same thing with this wild amount of money. If I told him I'd pay, I was certain he'd relax, stop bothering for a bit, and I could get him to either see reason or agree to a smaller amount. I bit my tongue to avoid fanning the flame of his anger even more. He knew that was a lot of money for me, and he was counting on me balking at the sum. He was hoping I'd say it was too much, and then we could get back to our obnoxious cycle of incessant calls and pressure for me to dump Juan. I had to agree if I wanted this all to stop. It was going to be a rough road, but if this was the way to get out of the mess with him, it was worth it—even if I had to figure out a way to wrangle together six thousand dollars.

"Fine. Six thousand dollars. And then you're out of my life."

"Deal. Just as soon as you give me my money."

Arnold knew I didn't have money, but he still put on a show, acting like he would try to help me earn the money. He offered to drive me to the mall and other stores so I could put in applications for jobs. All the while, he dominated my time on the phone, constantly pressing me for the money—even though he knew exactly what my financial situation was and that I was jobless—and groping me whenever we were in the car together. Our phone calls were still long and so very hostile. There was yelling, anger, swearing, tearing into one another, and saying every awful thing either of us could think of as soon as it crossed our minds.

"Do you have my money?"

"No, douchebag. You know I don't."

"Maybe I just need to call Chunti. Let him in on a few secrets you've been keeping from him."

"Shut up, I'm trying to get you your money."

Every day, our conversations went like this. "Do you have my money?" *No.* "Are you going to get it to me?" *I don't owe you anything.* "Pay me or I tell Juan." Day in, day out there was so much noise, so much chaos, so much stress.

I didn't care about hurting him anymore, and he clearly didn't care about hurting me. I don't know if I thought I could say something mean enough to get him to back off, but it definitely felt great to finally release some anger in his direction. I hoped that agreeing to pay him six thousand dollars would earn me some peace or allow me to talk him down to something more reasonable, but I soon realized he wouldn't let go of this easily. I don't know if it was because of my age, the growing animosity between us, or the fact that I was talking to other guys, but when I agreed to pay Arnold, it only made him more obsessive.

I couldn't find work anywhere, and I knew the idea of me finding the money was ludicrous. I spent countless hours trying to get him to understand or agree to a smaller sum, trying to keep Juan in my life without letting him know what was really going on behind the scenes, and trying to make my parents as happy as I could with my performance in college. I thought things were insane during my senior year of high school, but compared to my life after high school, that year had been peaceful. I had nowhere to go for a moment of quiet, and I felt like everyone was pressuring me for something more—all the while I was trying to tend to this deep mortal wound inflicted on me over years of abuse. Finally, I cracked.

"I don't have your money, douchebag. Six thousand is too much, and you know it."

Arnold scoffed, "Listen, it's what you owe me."

"Well, I can't pay it. So back off."

"I've wasted years on you. I've put up with so much crap from you, so I deserve some recognition for that."

"Yeah, you've been awesome. Let me just applaud you for the way you've made my life hell since I was fourteen."

"Don't try to twist this, Cindy! You knew what you were doing. You're not stupid. You've always been smart. You knew exactly what you could get from me. And now that I'm too inconvenient for you, you're dropping me. Real class act. I deserve some payment after the years I wasted trying to keep you around."

"Well, six thousand bucks is crazy. I can't find a job, so there's no way I can pay you. So you're just going to have to stop bothering me about it, be a man, and move on."

"No. That's not fair and you know it, Cindy. I deserve something, and if you can't pay me with cash, then you can pay me with sex."

My stomach dropped. How did I not see that coming? Of course that was his next move. My mind raced as I tried to figure out what to do.

"I'm not having sex with you."

"Then give me six thousand dollars. Or Chunti is gonna find out everything."

I hung up the phone, my ears ringing. He had me right where he wanted. He had laid another trap, and I had fallen right into it. He demanded more money than I had ever had in my life or sex—or Juan would find out the truth about why I was pushing him away. Tears stung my eyes as my heartbeat increased, panic slowly settling in.

I knew I would never be able to pay him. *Never.* Even if I did find a job, it would take me years to earn enough to pay him off. Day after day, I fielded calls from him where he demanded I either pay him or sleep with him. There wasn't another option, and he wasn't letting up. If anything, his demands were getting more incessant. I think the realization that he had me backed into a corner got him excited, and he knew I was close to breaking. So he kept pushing.

"Where's my money?"

"I don't have it."

"Then you can pay me in sex."

"No!"

"Then where's my money?"

"I don't have it."

It was yet another tireless cycle of manipulation that I couldn't escape. As he could feel my resolve weakening, he laid it on even thicker. When I woke up, my phone would be brimming with voicemails and texts from him. Sometimes, my phone lit up with a notification from him and stirred me from sleep. I left my phone off for a few hours to get a little peace, but the second I turned it back on, my phone would go nuts catching up with all of the missed calls, voicemails, and texts. Arnold could feel me pulling away, but he also knew this was a great way to keep me on the hook. He was getting desperate, frantic, and I could feel it when I read his texts and listened to his voicemails—his emotions were flying all over the place.

"Where's my money, Cindy? I'm tired of waiting! Money or sex but make a choice *now*."

"I don't know why you're hurting me like this. Why are you doing this? I just want to take care of you."

"I'm tired of waiting, bitch. Pay me now. You owe me big and you know it. I'm a vengeful person, and I don't like to be kept waiting like this. You don't want to see what happens."

"Don't you understand? I'm so lonely. I sold my boat. It's just me and my dog. I just want you to love me and see how much I love you."

"I'm calling Chunti. I'm tired of waiting."

"I'm sorry. I don't know what I did to make you treat me this way, but whatever it is, I'm sorry."

"You're a slut!"

"You're my soul mate."

"I love you."

"I hate you."

"I just want to take care of you."

"I want what's best for you."

All of this sent me into a spiral of panic and anxiety so intense it felt like my skin was on fire. Every sound around me was too loud. Every light was too bright. Every ounce of food I tried to eat was too flavorful and too filling. I didn't want to see anything, hear anything, touch anything, or eat anything. The way Arnold was harassing me had monopolized my brain and my heart so much that I didn't have the capacity to take in anything else.

I felt like I was trapped with Arnold. I was ruining my relationship with Juan, though he had no idea what was driving us apart. And in the midst of it all, my mother kept hassling me about college. She told me I wasn't taking enough credits, she wasn't happy with the school I chose, and she didn't understand why I wouldn't just get a job and start bringing in real money. Every day, I felt like someone was reminding me about one of the various ways I failed or disappointed them. I couldn't see any way to get the noise to stop. Every time I sat alone in my room, my thoughts would be ringing with my parents' criticism, concern from Juan, and the desperate ravings of Arnold. And if I managed to quiet my mind for a moment, my phone would buzz me back into reality.

"Give me my money or give me your body."

"Why are you doing this to me?"

"I'm outside. I see Juan's car just left your house. Maybe I should follow him home and pay him a visit."

"I just want to take care of you, Cindy. Please understand."

"You just don't know what you want, and you're too shallow to see how good I am for you."

"I wish you wouldn't hurt me so much."

"Give me my money now or give me what I deserve. You owe me that much."

"You can't pay me back for everything I gave you, so you can at least give me what I've got coming to me. It's time to pay up, Cindy."

"I wish I didn't have to bribe you to get you to sleep with me. Don't you see I just want to love you?"

"Your body is mine. You owe me, and you know it's true. Give me my money or give me sex; I'm tired of you jerking me around like this."

"Why won't you let me be there for you?"

"I hate you."

"You're beautiful."

"Maybe I just need to talk to Chunti."

"I love you so much, Cindy; please just listen to me."

"If you were dead, I could just have you stuffed and then I could have sex with you whenever I wanted."

Finally, I had enough. I spent nearly two weeks having every quiet moment filled with his voice, endless text notifications, voicemails filled with threats. I couldn't take it anymore, and I gave into his awful demands. I didn't want to, but I couldn't go one more day under such intense pressure and scrutiny. I thought that maybe if I told him what he wanted to hear, he'd back off. Maybe he wouldn't keep hounding me about sex; he'd just let me have some space and some quiet. And at first, it did change his mood. He instantly became really bright and cheery and said that we could figure out a time and place to get together. I hoped the cheerful mood would keep him away from me a bit, maybe even distract him from getting something concrete on our calendars.

Of course, that wasn't the case. Almost instantly, he started bugging me about arranging a time to meet. I put him off as long as I could, until he finally set a time and a date for me to come to his place. He was living in a house near my college rather than the tiny boat, but it was still a far cry from the house of the rich, affluent man my mother envisioned. I walked in the door in a panic, as if I were walking straight to my own execution. How had I gotten myself into such an awful mess? I looked around and tried to distract him.

"Want to get some food? Maybe we can watch a movie!"

"Stop that, Cindy. You know why you're here. It's time to pay up."

My stomach dropped. I felt like I was going to pass out or be sick. I started to feel lightheaded as my brain fought to find a way out of this, but there was none. Then I looked over at him and gasped: he was sitting on the couch, exposing himself. I was so overwhelmed with everything happening, the look on my face must have been one of utter disgust, because he instantly got upset.

He whined, "I don't understand why you aren't attracted to me after everything we've been through—after everything I've done for you. I don't know why you are so openly disgusted with me. Can't you see how good I am to you? How good I've been for you? C'mon, why don't you wipe that look off your face and come over here."

He kept trying to guilt me into feeling some kind of attraction to him and tried to get me aroused by continuing to expose himself. Of course, it just made me feel more scared and trapped, so he told me to give him oral sex. Frantic, I tried to distract him again, saying we should watch a movie or get some food.

But my tactics were futile, as he had one thing on his mind. He led me into his room. I thought maybe once he got a good look at me and how I looked that day, he wouldn't be attracted to me anymore. Before I came to his house, I had made sure to make myself as unattractive as possible: I didn't take any care with my hair or dress nicely, I barely put on any makeup so I could feel comfortable when I was in class prior to coming to his house, and I didn't shave. But he was blind to it all. My ears started ringing as he started to touch me, kiss me, and peel off my clothes. I tried to push him away a few times, but I knew it wouldn't do any good. I was trapped. I was screaming inside, but I knew there wasn't anyone who could help me.

Arnold noticed almost immediately that I hadn't shaved, and he made a comment about it. I hoped it would turn him off, but of course rape isn't about attraction. It's about power, and he was desperate to dominate me and keep me under his control. So, before he did anything else, he said he wanted to shave my privates. As he laid me down and shaved me, shame overwhelmed me. When he finished, he began giving me oral sex. I just laid there, lifeless and numb. I was terrified and heartbroken, and I didn't think there was any way for me to get him to stop this—now or ever.

With every second that passed, I started to feel more and more like a ghost, floating above my empty shell of a body that lay completely at the mercy of a ruthless abuser, unable to do anything except endure it. I felt ashamed, worthless, helpless. I couldn't stop berating myself for getting into such an awful situation, but I quickly realized I couldn't do anything to stop him from whatever he wanted to do to me that day. Worse yet, unlike the other times he raped me, I felt absolutely *certain* that I asked for it. After all, we set a date—this was on my calendar. I knew what he wanted to do to me, and I still made time in my schedule. My mom had been right all along—I was a slut.

Eventually, he moved onto having sex with me, and he pounded his body into mine for what felt like an eternity. I still felt as though I was floating above my body, almost like I'd died and couldn't feel anything. Of course, he didn't care. Just like all of the other times, he wasn't interested in me. He was focused on his own pleasure, his own sick feelings of conquest. In his mind, he was taking what was owed him—all of me.

When he was done, he drove me home. As I cried silent tears and stared out the window, agonizing over what a despicable person I must be, he interrupted my self-deprecation and said, "You could've at least acted like you enjoyed it. You're such a cold fish."

I didn't even look at him, but I couldn't believe how cavalier he was about it all. Here I was, visibly distraught and broken, and he thought giving me notes was a good move. And worse yet, it implied the more sinister idea that this wouldn't be the last time. I pushed that thought out of my mind.

When I got home, I walked straight to the shower and cried. I tried my best to wash away the feeling of him, but I knew that no matter how hard I scoured, I could never get rid of him; he was like an invisible residue. My actions had sullied me, I was a dirty person, and I wouldn't ever be able to be clean again. I was disgusting and too far gone to ever be saved.

When I got out of the shower, my phone lit up. I looked at the screen, and my stomach dropped. It was Arnold. I didn't have the energy to talk with him, so I ignored the call. But he quickly sent me the text: *Call me.*

With the little energy I could muster, I called him back. If I didn't, I knew he wouldn't leave me alone. He didn't waste any time with formalities.

"So, I just wanted to let you know how we're going to do this to take care of everything you owe me."

My mind raced. I thought we were square. Hadn't I paid him back today?

"We're gonna do this about two or three times a week for a while until you've paid me back the six grand you owe me."

I felt like I was going to throw up, and I cried out in a voice that was so loud I surprised myself, "No! That was it!"

Arnold responded in a totally matter-of-fact tone, as if I were settling a debt with the bank. "No, one time isn't even close to making up for the six grand you owe me. So we're going to have to do this a lot more. I'm thinking two or three times a week. Make time in your schedule, pay me what you owe, or I'm talking to Chunti."

I steadied myself on the sink, my whole body trembled at the thought of having to do this again—and again and again. I wanted to scream or cry, but what was the point? Yet again, I had put myself in a compromising position, and I had to deal with the consequences. But I knew I couldn't bear another rape, so I yelled frantically that I wasn't going to sleep with him again.

Of course, that catapulted me back into the dizzying cycle of him harassing me, demanding sex or money. As time passed, if he wasn't with me or on the phone with me, he was stalking me and stalking Juan. I still didn't truly know what he was capable of, but I knew he was incredibly dangerous. So, like I had before, I tried to break the cycle. I tried to get him to stop, but my efforts were in vain. Once again, I woke up to a flurry of texts, voicemails, and missed calls. My phone became practically unusable throughout the day because of how much he harassed me. Like a refrain on repeat, his threats, put-downs, and pleas echoed constantly in my head. I couldn't turn him off. It was too much.

I can't remember exactly how long I was able to take his obsessive calls, but it felt like an eternity. I just couldn't take it anymore. Exhausted and out of options, I agreed to his terms in the hopes of getting some peace. He told me to act a little more into it than last time, but once again, I felt like I left my body during the duration of the attack as I lay there, lifeless. I didn't know how my life had turned into this hell, and I was starting to wonder if it would ever end. Every time I tried to tell him no, he found a way to creep back into my life. Every time I put up a boundary, he slowly chipped away at my sanity until I had no options left but to agree to his sickening terms. I felt that every time he touched me, a little bit of my heart shattered into new pieces. I was wholly broken, hopeless, and disgusted with myself, and it showed on my face. The rapes were all about him and what he could take from me. At that point, I felt like he had taken just about everything.

I knew if I wanted to keep living, I couldn't carry on with this abuse.

So, I told him definitively that I refused to let him touch me again, and he reverted to pestering me about the money. Once again, I racked my brain to find a way out or figure out how to silence his voice in my head and stop the phone calls. But things were about to change in a way I could never have anticipated. I found out I was pregnant with Juan's baby.

CHAPTER SEVEN
UNEXPECTED TWIST

When I officially found out I was pregnant and noticed my period was late, I almost wanted to laugh. I was stuck in the middle of the wildest, most all-encompassing hellish period of my life. My parents' hostility toward me progressed every day, I was struggling my way through college classes, and I was keeping my relationship with the man I loved afloat by the skin of my teeth—all the while being blackmailed and threatened by a man who raped and assaulted me multiple times. Why wouldn't an unplanned pregnancy be plopped on top of all of that mess? The only silver lining was that it had been a few months since Arnold had raped me, so I knew for certain that if I was indeed pregnant, the baby could only be Juan's.

As the days passed and my period still didn't come, I realized I needed to tell Juan what was going on. His face went a bit pale when I told him I might be pregnant, and we hurried along to a clinic to get a pregnancy test. I took the test as soon as we arrived, and Juan and I were told to wait in an exam room for the results. We didn't talk a lot while we were waiting. The thought of bringing a child into the world terrified both of us. Neither of us had stable jobs or money, and even though I was nineteen and Juan was twenty, we were still very much kids. How were we supposed to be someone's parents? I silently prayed that the test would come back negative, hoping that maybe I had missed a period because I was so stressed.

A nurse came into the room with a big smile on her face and said, "Congratulations!"

At first, I thought she was congratulating us because the test was negative, so I let out a huge sigh of relief.

"You're going to be parents!"

The nurse could tell from the looks on our faces that wasn't exactly the news we were hoping to hear. She muttered a quick apology and promised to give us a minute to talk. As soon as she left the room, I burst into tears. It was too much for me to handle—I was completely drowning in my own life circumstances. I couldn't care for myself in any real way, and I was suddenly supposed to bring a child into the world? I was supposed to be a parent? How was this even fair?! When would I catch a bit of a break?

Juan put his hand on my shoulder and said, "I know this isn't what either of us expected, but I want you to know that I'm going to take responsibility. This child is as much mine as it is yours, and I'm going to be there for both of you. I promise."

Weakly, with a tear-stained face, I smiled at him and leaned in for a hug. Cautiously, the nurse came back into the room.

"Have we had a minute to talk things through?"

"Yes, thanks," Juan said.

"So, what are you two going to do?"

"What do you mean?" I asked.

"It's pretty obvious that this isn't a planned pregnancy. Are you going to terminate?"

Juan and I both shook our heads, and I said, "No, of course not. We're going to have this baby."

The pregnancy was unexpected and we felt unprepared, but we weren't about to walk away. For once, I was able to look ahead to a huge challenge, link arms with someone, and know I wouldn't have to face it alone. Despite being scared and overwhelmed, having Juan by my side made it seem a little less terrifying. We drove home in silence. Neither of us knew what to do next, and we were still trying to wrap our minds around our new reality. I knew I couldn't tell my parents, and I had no idea how Juan's parents would react. I was certain they'd all hate me.

Juan broke the silence, saying, "Listen, I'll break the news to my mom. She's going to be mad, and I think I should face the brunt of that. We'll start there, and we can make plans on what to do next once that's behind me."

I nodded. At the time, I wasn't terribly close with his mom, but I knew she was both nice and completely terrifying. She would not be happy to hear that her son had gotten his girlfriend pregnant when they weren't married and didn't have any source of reliable income. I couldn't help but breathe a sigh of relief that I wouldn't be the one to inform her. However, when I was at my house, I did my best to keep it a secret. At about two months pregnant, I started getting really bloated—and my mom and sister definitely noticed something. They also witnessed my weird cravings.

"If you're having a piece of trash," my mom warned, "then I'm going to drag you out into the street and tell all of the neighbors what trash *you* are. And I will beat senseless that piece of trash who got you pregnant."

I was terrified, and Juan and I started talking about ways to keep the baby and me safe. At the very least, staying at home with my parents was damaging to my mental health and that degree of stress was toxic for me and the baby.

But all of that paled in comparison to the moment Arnold found out. I don't know what I expected from him, but the cruelty he displayed when

I told him still shocked me. Arnold was furious that I was pregnant with Juan's baby and continued to lay on the guilt trip about me "cheating" on him with Juan. But the biggest shock was that he started pressuring me to get an abortion.

"You're going to get an abortion, right, Cindy?"

"Of course not!"

Arnold sighed and grumbled. "Oh, you Hispanics are outrageous! You think it's just so cute to have a baby, to have the big baby shower, and you guys get knocked up left and right and have all of these kids running around that no one can afford or care for! C'mon, Cindy! You can't think this is a good idea! You know having Chunti's kid is wild, right?"

"I'm sorry, *what* did you just say to me?"

"You heard me! You're just like every other Hispanic out there, ready to pop out kids and then go on welfare or whatever to get the state to take care of them. This is a big deal, Cindy, and you know you're not ready for a baby. You know you don't want Juan's kid. You've got to get an abortion."

Suddenly, it was as if the distorted lens through which Arnold made me see the world had been smashed. It wasn't just about me and my suffering anymore; we were talking about my unborn child. And something instinctual deep inside of me woke up—and it was utterly feral. This man was not about to tell me what I needed to do with my child, and he was not about to even hint at harming my baby.

"You don't get to tell me to get an abortion. This is my baby, and I'm keeping it. So you can just wrap your mind around that fact or keep your thoughts to yourself. But you don't get a say over what happens to my baby, you douche."

Arnold laughed. "Wow! Okay, well then what do you say I have a little talk with Chunti and let him know what his whore of a baby momma's been doing with me? You think he's going to feel as passionate as you are when he finds out about me? About us?"

"There is no *us*."

"I bet Chunti would disagree with that."

"Screw you."

"Listen, Cindy. I'll make it easy for you. You get rid of that baby, or I'm telling him everything. I'm done playing with you about this one. I've put up with enough of your crap, and this is the last straw. You get an abortion, or he finds out."

I hung up the phone in disbelief. This felt like a new low, even for him. But more than ever, I was terrified of Juan finding out. Of course the first thing Juan would think when he found out about Arnold was that the baby was Arnold's, not his. And losing Juan wouldn't just be heartbreaking. With a baby on the way, having to walk this road all by myself would be devastating, and I wasn't totally sure I could do it on my own. Did my baby really deserve to live a life with one parent because her mom was molested by a substitute teacher and that truth drove my baby's father away? And if Juan walked, who would ever be interested in me after that? I'd lose the love of my life, my baby's father. I'd be damaged goods and on my own forever.

Or worse, I'd spend the rest of my life with Kip Arnold. The thought of Arnold raising my child flashed through my mind for a quick second, making me gag. I resolved that I would never let that monster anywhere near my child. But for now, I had to determine my next steps.

Mercifully, the pregnancy had distracted him from hounding me about the money or paying him back with sex. However, he was just as demanding about the abortion as he was about paying off my supposed debt. I couldn't find a moment of peace, and with the added pressure of an unplanned pregnancy (and those delightful pregnancy hormones), everything felt ten thousand times worse.

My parents' animosity, my performance in college, my job prospects, and my future now were not only deep cuts to my own sense of worth, but they were also threats to the safety and wellbeing of my unborn child. How could I ever expect my kid to live a happy, healthy life if I couldn't get my own life together? How could I even think about being a good mom if I was the childish, selfish, manipulative, shallow person that my mother and Arnold led me to believe I was?

I knew I couldn't continue living like this. I wasn't sure what I could do (if anything) to fix things with my parents, especially as I could no longer effectively hide my pregnancy. But the next time I was on the phone with Arnold, I realized how I could get some peace, at least from him.

"Have you scheduled an abortion yet?" Arnold demanded.

I drew a deep breath. "No, I haven't. You know I don't want to do that."

"I don't know how many more ways I can say this, Cindy. You need to do it. You're too young. You don't know what you want, and your hormones aren't letting you see straight. But this isn't going to be good for you or any baby you manage to bring into the world with *him*."

"I don't think it's right and you know it. Juan and I can provide this baby with a loving home; I know we can."

"Oh, you Hispanics are all alike. You get so starry-eyed over a baby, and then when the kid actually comes out and needs to be taken care of, you all don't know what to do."

"That's not true!"

"I can see how that might offend you with your perfect, loving, supportive parents."

"Shut up, douchebag. You don't get to talk about my parents, especially not that way."

Arnold laughed bitterly. "I'm just repeating what I've heard from you. And honestly, if the train wreck of your life with your folks hasn't scared you away from having a baby, I don't know what will. I'm telling you: you are too young to see it and your hormones have you confused. But this isn't good; it's not right, and it's not what you want. I know it isn't, and deep down, you do too. You just haven't been able to admit it to yourself yet. You need to schedule an abortion. And if you don't, I'm going to tell Juan about us. Are these morals of yours worth having to raise this kid on your own?"

I drew my breath in slowly, trying to calm myself down. I was already terrified of this pregnancy, but I knew I couldn't live with myself if I got an abortion. And something about raising a baby with Juan felt right to me. It felt beautiful and hopeful, even though this pregnancy was unplanned. But I realized I could get Arnold to leave me alone if I just told him what he wanted to hear. I could sort out the repercussions later and having even one night free from his nagging would help me think straight and start making a plan.

"You're right," I blurted.

"I'm sorry, what?" Arnold balked.

"You're right. This is crazy. I'm too young. I don't know what I want."

"What are you saying, Cindy?"

"I'm saying I'll do it."

"You'll get the abortion?"

"Yes."

Instantly, Arnold's tone changed. He sounded brighter, happier, relieved, and even a bit excited. "Oh, that's great! You're making the right choice, Cindy. See? You just didn't know what you wanted. You needed me to help you see straight to find the right choice. I'm relieved that you're finally listening to reason."

Although it might have sounded like I was complicit, bending yet again to Arnold's demands, this time was different. I didn't realize it then, but something inside me changed in that moment. He sparked a flame within me that would become a blazing inferno in the months and years to come. For the first time, I was standing up for myself. I was finding my voice. Sure, I just told Arnold what he wanted to hear, but I made a conscious choice to defy him. There was no way in hell the man could make me get an abortion. This wouldn't be like on the boat or those times in his house. He wouldn't trick me, he wouldn't overpower me, and he wouldn't back me into a corner. We were talking about my unborn child, and I wasn't about to let Arnold have any sort of influence on my baby. Then, the day after I told Arnold I'd get an abortion, he called to check up on me.

"So, have you gotten an abortion yet?"

I sighed. I knew this was coming, but hearing his voice dampened my hope. Still, I tried to distract him in an attempt to buy myself a few more days of silence.

"Not yet. I've got a lot on my plate right now."

He let out a sharp sigh. "You're scared."

"Of course, I'm scared, but I'm also very busy. So, relax."

He sighed again. "Listen, I knew the only way this was going to get done was if I took over. You just never know what you want, so let me do what's best for you."

"What does that mean?"

"I'm going to make you an appointment to have the procedure. That way you can't get cold feet or start thinking you might want to have this baby. I'm going to schedule it, and it'll be really easy. You're so early in your pregnancy, it should be simple. You can just take a pill, and it'll be over. You won't even feel a thing."

I shut my eyes and squeezed until I started to see stars, and then I took a deep breath. *Just tell him what he wants to hear.*

I threw up my hands in frustration. "Yeah, sure, do whatever you want."

"Great! I'll make the appointment right away."

After we hung up, panic set in. I knew I was nearing the end of being able to string him along. But I wasn't about to get an abortion just to keep Arnold happy. This was bigger than me—bigger than the hold he had over me for so many years. My maternal instincts were starting to kick in, fanning the flames of strength and self-confidence. And though the light was still small, I refused to allow Arnold to snuff it out.

Since I didn't intend to follow through with his demands, I needed a plan. He was still stalking me, so even though he hadn't touched me since the last time he raped me, he was always close. I had no idea what he might do if I told him I planned to have the baby. Would he hurt me? Would he try to hurt the baby? Would he hurt Juan? My family? Juan's family? Would he just tell Juan what he did to me and watch the fallout happen? The possibilities of ways Arnold could destroy my life seemed endless, but I started to realize that I had the power to get away from him.

Arnold didn't waste time making an appointment for an abortion, but he needed my medical insurance card. So he called me back that same day and asked for the information. Once that happened, I knew things had gone far enough, and I refused.

"Are you kidding me?! We talked about this! You're not ready to be a mom. Chunti's not ready to be a dad. You two aren't fit to be parents, and it's time you finally realize what a loser Juan is, drop him, and see what a good man you've got in me. Whether he goes because I tell him the truth or he just gets bored with you, you're going to be left alone—this time with a kid—and you'll have nowhere to turn. But I'll still be there, waiting. I'll always be there. Why can't you see that?"

And for the first time ever, I truly did—just not how he wanted me to see it. I was still terrified, unable to silence the voices of self-doubt and fear ringing in my mind. But I put my foot down: Arnold *would not* hurt my child.

"I'm not giving you my insurance info."

"Cindy, I know you're scared of the procedure. I told you, you just have to take a pill. It's not gonna—"

"You're not listening to me. I'm *not* giving you the information because I'm *not* having an abortion. And that's final."

My heart pounded in my chest as I hung up the phone. That was the first time I used my voice—the first time I spoke my truth, rocked the boat, and told someone that *I* knew best and that they were wrong. And I believed it, but I trembled with fear as I thought about Arnold's response. I was proud of myself for standing up to him, but from that moment on, I constantly felt on edge about Arnold showing up out of the blue to wreak havoc in my life.

Around the same time, Juan and I realized there was no way I'd be able to survive my pregnancy living with my parents. I had moved out a few months prior because my relationship with my mother had become so toxic that we couldn't live together. I ultimately moved back home, but that brief time away had opened up my world a bit. Moving out showed me that I could live a better life away from my parents, a living situation where I didn't have to spend every waking moment in fear of their constant criticism and scrutiny.

That tiny flame within me started to grow a bit stronger.

If I continued living with my parents during my pregnancy, then their spitefulness would break me—the cracks about my changing body, the attacks on my and Juan's characters, and the horrible predictions of what a bad mom I'd be. And that wasn't even looping Arnold into the situation. It became pretty clear that I would have to make some big changes.

My focus had shifted; I wasn't just thinking about myself. I was concerned about the future of my child and the choices I would make about building my family. I knew one thing for sure: I didn't want my child to grow up in a toxic family environment like I had. So I knew I would have to start making some bold choices and trusting my instincts, despite my parents repeatedly telling me that my instincts were wrong and only led me to make bad decisions.

I decided to move in with Juan's family.

Juan's mother was, as expected, furious when Juan told her I was pregnant. But she didn't kick Juan out, she didn't call me a slut, and she didn't turn hostile. Instead, she offered to let us move into their home. I still wasn't close with Juan's family at all, but I knew I had no other choice. My mom and my sister became more suspicious as time wore on, making jokes about my weight and the possibility of me "having a piece of trash" with Juan. So Juan and I started making plans for the move.

We realized it probably wasn't a good idea to announce that I was leaving, especially because I half expected to hear my parents respond to my "I'll be moving out next month" with "Nope. You're out of the family. Get out now." Instead, we figured it would be easier for everyone if I just moved out and explained to my parents after it was all over. We hoped tensions wouldn't be as high and that I would feel safer telling the truth about the pregnancy.

When I was about eight weeks pregnant, Juan and I decided it was time.

And with the tension I experienced after shutting Arnold down, I knew it was time to take drastic steps to extricate Arnold from my life for good. We had to plan everything carefully for the move to happen seamlessly. We waited until my mother was at work, and I tried to make sure Arnold wasn't around, following us. I knew Arnold had given himself access to my cell phone account by creating an online profile, too. If I wanted to give him the slip, I couldn't just move; I needed to get rid of my phone. So I didn't just turn it off forever or remove the SIM card. I smashed it.

My heart raced as I stared at the shattered phone. Seeing it in pieces on the ground felt so freeing because I was looking at the wreckage of the main way Arnold had crept into my life. He used my phone to gain access to me at home; it was the first and most effective way he manipulated me, how he convinced my mother to be on his side, and the method through which he made my life a living hell for years. I looked up, tears stinging the edges of my eyelids. *Years.* It had been years—time I would never get back, time when I felt like a puppet under his control. By breaking the phone, I felt like I was finally breaking free from the puppet master. I didn't know how long this euphoria would last—I didn't expect years of fear, shame, and guilt simply to melt away—so I didn't waste time getting ready to make my escape.

My sister saw me preparing to move and became furious.

"What do you think you're doing? You're moving out? You're just going to leave your family? What a slap in the face to the people who have taken care of you for all these years! And you're going to move in with Juan like a slut? I can't believe you! I can't believe you're doing this while Mom is at work! I'm calling her right now to tell her to come over here and knock some sense into you!"

Juan and I worked as fast as we could to move my stuff out of the house, but things came to a halt when my father came home and saw what we were doing.

"So you're moving out?"

My eyes filled with tears. "Yes."

My dad nodded; his expression was inscrutable. I couldn't tell if he was furious, heartbroken, or maybe a bit of both. He scratched his face, clearly mulling over the situation, then cleared his throat and nodded again, "Alright, Cindy. You want to move out, fine. You go. Go live with Juan. Leave us. Do what you want, just like you always do."

I opened my mouth to protest, and he held up a finger. "But let me tell you this. If you walk out that door with him, you're gone. You leave your key, and you say your goodbyes to this place forever. Because this isn't going to be like the last time you moved out. If you leave here, you're gone for good. Do you hear what I'm saying? No moving back. You walk out that door right now, just know you're walking out for good."

A tear escaped from the corner of my eye. I drew in a deep breath and cleared my throat to choke back a sob. I nodded, took my house key off the key ring, placed it on the counter, walked out the door, and closed it behind me. My heart dropped as I heard my dad lock the door behind me.

I was silent on the ride to Juan's house, and he could tell how conflicted I felt. He gently squeezed my hand and smiled at me. "It's going to be okay; I promise."

I looked at him and smiled weakly. As I turned to stare out the window, I couldn't stop myself from stealing glances in the rearview mirror. I felt so many emotions all at once—heartbreak at my dad's words, elation to finally be free from Arnold and my toxic home life, and terror that Arnold was looking for me. I knew Arnold must have wondered why I wasn't answering his calls. I hadn't seen him outside my house, but sometimes he was really good at hiding or used a different car to blend in more effectively. I attempted to concentrate on breathing, keeping calm, and feeling excited for this new future. But every time I tried to relax and relish my newfound sense of freedom as I watched the sun dip over the California skyline, my eyes would almost involuntarily dart to a rearview mirror to check for Arnold. As if, among the breathtakingly beautiful hues of pink and purple and orange, his silhouette would appear—sinister, looming, darkening everything.

CHAPTER EIGHT
SPEAKING UP

Moving into Juan's home was a huge culture shock for me. I suddenly had to learn how to become a functioning member of a household rather than someone who spent most of her days alone in her room. I had a partner to support and a home to build for the two of us and our future child. And all the while, I had the constant creeping fear that one day I'd be out with Juan—or Juan and our baby—and see Arnold's hulking figure hovering over us.

    I tried my best to not think about him, reminding myself that I had broken my phone, made sure he wasn't following us, and moved out of my house quickly enough that Arnold didn't have the chance to catch wind of my plans. But I also knew it wouldn't take a huge mental leap for him to conclude that I had moved in with Juan's family. Every time I fell asleep, I attempted to push away fears that we would wake up in the middle of the night and find him standing in our room or that I would walk outside one morning and see his car parked out front. Every time a blocked or private number would call my phone, my heart would start pounding in my ears. I didn't answer those calls—I held my breath, waiting to see if they left a voicemail for me. When they didn't, I often wondered if it was actually Arnold or just some telemarketer. Nothing made me feel more relief than seeing a voicemail notification and hearing, "We've been trying to contact you about your vehicle's factory warranty." I was constantly looking over my shoulder, having mild panic attacks every time my phone buzzed, and making sure our doors were securely locked at night to hopefully stop Arnold if he tried to barge in the house in the middle of the night.

After all, over the years Arnold seemed to pop up everywhere, just to let me know he was watching. And I couldn't help replaying his "joke" about having me stuffed "if I was dead," or the warning he gave me that seemed like a lifetime ago. "I am a very vengeful person," he threatened, and I believed him. I had no idea what he might do now that I had escaped his grasp and was planning to have the baby—the baby he so furiously wanted me to abort.

Despite my fears, I never saw Arnold and his number never popped up on my phone. However, he did make sure I knew that he was still around. My nephew was actually attending the school where Arnold worked, and Arnold recognized him pretty quickly. He didn't waste time trying to strike up a conversation with my nephew. Arnold asked him about me, and though my nephew didn't give Arnold a lot of information about my living situation, he did deliver a message to me.

"Mr. Arnold talked to me about you today. It was kinda weird. He wanted to know what you were doing and where you were living and stuff," my nephew said.

My blood ran cold as I tried to keep my tone neutral. "What did you tell him?"

My nephew shrugged, "I dunno, not much. I said you weren't living at home anymore and that I don't really see you as much because you're living with someone else now."

"And what did Mr. Arnold say?"

"Nothing really. Oh, I guess he did tell me to tell you that he's around and you should call him sometime."

My ears started ringing and I couldn't help but frantically look behind me. Was he watching me right then? I checked my phone, certain I had felt it buzzing, but I realized that was only my imagination. I couldn't see him or his car anywhere. I strained my eyes to look as far into the distance as I could but still didn't see him. This extreme panic sent me reeling and all I wanted to do was run. Had he been following my nephew to see where I was? To catch a glimpse of me? Was he planning on kidnapping me? Hurting Juan? Hurting my family? Was he going to do something to my nephew to get to me?

I tried my best to look at the facts. As far as I could tell, Arnold wasn't anywhere to be seen. He hadn't called me. I hadn't seen him outside of Juan's parents' house, and I hadn't seen him driving behind us. But he was around. And he wanted me to know it.

I'm a very vengeful person.
Call me sometime.
I'm around.

His words shook me to my core, but I knew one thing for certain: I refused to allow him back into my life. I had a child on the way, and there was no possible scenario where I'd let him anywhere near my child. I just needed to lay low, watch my back, and protect my family. I was certain that he'd either lose interest or finally give up on trying to find me. Either way, I hoped that if I kept my head down long enough, the threat would pass, and my family (and the secret of what he did to me) would be safe.

With the exception of the terror of Arnold finding me, my pregnancy went on without a hitch, and the birth went smoothly as well. I had a beautiful daughter, and Juan and I were over the moon in love with her. Life with a newborn can be tough—especially when you don't have any real money, are trying to build the foundation of a life together, and are still living with your parents. Juan's parents let us turn their garage into a little apartment, so we finally had our own space, but we still relied on them for a lot of support.

Juan's mom quickly began to fill that motherly role for me. She was tough, but she cared about us and genuinely wanted to help us succeed. I felt increasingly comfortable talking with her, learning how to cook and clean, and even asking her for advice. And though she didn't suffer any nonsense, she was usually pretty open to talking. She knew we struggled for money, so she and Juan's dad even helped us with a few bills and often made us food.

My mother frequently told my sister and me that she was cold with us as a mother because she couldn't give us the love and affection that had never been shown to her. And that idea terrified me when I thought of my own daughter. Would that cycle continue with me, and would I be as cold to my kids because I didn't receive affection from my parents? Thankfully, the time I spent with Juan's family opened my eyes to the many ways a family could show one another love, appreciation, and affection. The more time I spent with them, not only did I learn basic household skills, but I also learned to be a more loving, warm person and parent. Stepping outside of my own bubble and getting input, information, and the perspective of others helped me understand how to interact with people and be a part of a loving family.

That's the thing with abuse. Whether it's mental and verbal abuse or the grooming and sexual abuse I suffered at the hands of Kip Arnold, as long as the abuser can keep their victim from looking outside of themselves and their circumstances, they have a greater chance of keeping their own power intact. Once a survivor starts to look beyond their circumstances and the distorted truths they've been fed by those who abused them, they not only start to see the truth, but they also start to see hope. Arnold was able to worm his way into my life in such a profound manner because I was naturally inwardly focused—I was quiet, I didn't rock the boat, I processed my emotions internally more than verbally, and I thought speaking up caused more pain and problems than anything.

Arnold used all of that to manipulate and gaslight me into keeping that inward-focused perspective. And once the abuse started, that inward focus and self-preservation instinct became a huge beast that I had to fight to hide my fear, shame, and total lack of self-confidence. Arnold knew as long as I stayed in that frame of mind, I could easily be manipulated. If I buried my gut instincts, concerns, questions, fear, and shame, then I wouldn't ask someone for a second opinion. I wouldn't process an attack or a sexually explicit conversation with anyone else; I'd just keep it inside.

It was the perfect environment for abuse to fester and take total control over someone's life. Just as my parents knew that as long as they kept me feeling ashamed of my choices, contrite whenever I did something they didn't like, and convinced that my instincts were always wrong and theirs were right, I'd be easy to order around. Those factors had fashioned me into the perfect victim for an abuser like Arnold.

But once I realized there was life outside of myself and outside of my pain, everything changed. When I found out I was pregnant, suddenly my world got a lot bigger. My concerns for the well-being of my child caused me to see other outside perspectives. I understood that my family life was toxic. And when I thought about my daughter as a fourteen-year-old, I knew how wholly unacceptable everything Arnold had ever said or done to me truly was. That realization empowered me to find a way out.

Maybe I hadn't totally found my voice yet, and I was still too scared to speak the truth about what happened to me (and I still internalized all of the blame). But I was finally seeing how much life there was outside of Kip Arnold's grasp. Even if I wasn't quite free, I started to see faint rays of hope as each day passed and I didn't see or hear from Arnold. I believed more each day that I had found a way to escape Arnold and keep my life somewhat intact in the process.

Days turned into weeks, weeks to months, and months to years. Slowly but surely, I looked over my shoulder less and less. Arnold never showed up. He never called. I never saw him tailing us on the road or walking in the periphery while we were in public. I didn't spot him in crowds. For all intents and purposes, Kip Arnold was no longer a part of my life.

And for our part, Juan and I were beginning to build a life we were proud of. We had both dropped out of college to begin building our own financial consulting business. After a lot of hard work, we earned enough to start saving up to find a place of our own. We dreamed big about the life we wanted our daughter to lead. We started to think about how we wanted to prepare her for her future and what ways we could provide for her and any future kids if our business continued to thrive.

It was amazing. Finally, I felt like I was achieving some real success in my life. I was working hard and trusting my gut more every day—and it was paying off. Starting our business was my idea; Juan wasn't on board at first. My daughter's birth completely changed my outlook on life. I wasn't just trying to survive anymore; I was a mother. I had to create a life where my baby could thrive. I needed to achieve so she, and any other children Juan and I had in the future, could have a better life than I did.

But I was still hiding this dark, terrible secret. Even though I wasn't paranoid about seeing Kip Arnold everywhere I turned, his ghost and the repercussions of his actions haunted me. Every time I saw a larger man with a similar haircut out of the corner of my eye, my heart rate increased. If I smelled a cologne similar to his or any other odor that reminded me of his house or his boat, my fight or flight instincts kicked in. I didn't realize it but, although I had managed to find a way to escape from his influence, the unresolved trauma was destroying me from the inside out. I could feel the unsteadiness within me. Everything I wanted to build for my family and myself was shaky because I had built it on the rotting foundation of my trauma, guilt, shame, and fear.

But I did my best to ignore the pain. Just like turning your car radio up when you hear your engine making a funny sound, I decided to turn up the volume of everything else in my life to hide the rattling of my broken heart. Even though I wasn't as concerned about Kip Arnold showing up to tell Juan the truth, the thought of Juan finding out terrified me; I worried he would leave me. I loved Juan and the life we were creating together far too much to let that happen.

But one day, through Juan and my business, I met a girl who had gone to my old school. Her name was Melissa. She was younger than me, so I didn't have any past connection with her, but she mentioned she had an older sister, Marisol. The name clicked a vague memory. She was younger than me as well, but she was a student of Arnold's. I remembered seeing her name on papers I graded and class rosters when I helped him out around school. I could picture Marisol's face as Melissa and I reconnected. Eventually, we started talking about school, and somehow the topic made its way over to Mr. Arnold. Melissa made an errant comment about him being creepy that stopped me in my tracks. I tried to hold a good poker face, but I think Melissa could sense the sudden shift in my mood.

"What do you mean he was creepy?"

Melissa shrugged and sighed. "He was just really creepy with my sister."

I drew a deep breath. "Was she in his class or something? What did he do?"

Melissa sighed again. "Yeah, he was her teacher. Okay, I know this sounds awful, but try to just hear me out. I don't want you to jump to conclusions and think any less of Marisol. I guess one day he started asking her a lot of questions about herself. Her likes and dislikes, details about her family, stuff like that. And my sister was really into skating at the time, so they talked about that a lot. He asked her questions about it, and I guess at one point he even bought her a pair of new skates. He was going to take her skating with some other people, but my mom found out about it. She ripped him a new one and basically threatened him within an inch of his life if he didn't back off for good."

I stared at Melissa, my mouth agape.

Melissa cringed. "Look, I know people hear this stuff and their first question is about what she was doing, but you've got to understand, she was just a kid at the time. She didn't know any better. It wasn't her fault."

She was just a kid. Marisol was a couple of grades behind me, and from what Melissa said, it seemed like he tried to take her skating around the time I was moving on to high school. So he had tried to ensnare someone else at his school that he could see every day. It wasn't just me. I wasn't sure if I was the first student that he had abused, but I was horrified to realize I wasn't the last. I looked down and picked at my fingers, my heart racing. I could feel the words bubbling up in the back of my throat. Every fiber of my being was screaming at me to keep my mouth shut, but the words were coming up too strongly. I knew the truth was about to come spilling out, word-vomit style, and there was nothing I could do to stop it.

"He did it to me, too."

Melissa tilted her head. "What did you say?"

"He did it to me, too. But a lot worse. And for years."

Melissa opened her mouth to speak, closed it, shook her head, and then tried again. "Wait. You're saying he…he tried to give you stuff and take you out?"

Still looking at my hands, I started nodding furiously. "For starters." Slowly, I looked up at her. "You've got to understand, I've never told this to anyone else ever. Not even Juan. I don't even really know why I'm telling you now. But, Melissa, he's made my life hell. For years. It's been awful."

Melissa put her hand on my arm and gave me a light squeeze. "You don't have to talk about it if you don't want to, but if you want to talk, I'm listening."

My heart felt like it was about to beat right out of my chest. I wanted to keep it all inside. I didn't want anyone to know the truth about what had happened. I couldn't bear the shame or the judgment. But after years of hiding it any way I could, I had broken the seal. The truth had taken on a life of its own and had to come out. I held out hope that Melissa would at least be gracious when she heard my story and wait to talk about me until I was out of ear shot. And so, for the first time, I talked. I was too scared and ashamed to tell her everything, but I told her more than I had ever told anyone else. I told her he raped me. I told her he groomed me. I told her that he was undeniably dangerous, and she was right to be creeped out by him.

Even though I explained what he did to me in broad terms, finally speaking even a sliver of the truth rocked me to my core. I was a mess. I was ugly crying, my darkest secret spilling right into her lap, as I shared that part of my life aloud with another person for the first time ever. And to my surprise, I felt a little lighter. Don't get me wrong; it was horrifying to open up to her in such a vulnerable way, and I'm sure this heavy conversation was way more than Melissa bargained for that day. But I couldn't have asked for a better listener. When I finished telling her everything, as I tried to calm myself down and wipe the tears from my eyes, she just looked at me. And her eyes didn't hold the judgment or anger I expected; I saw concern and empathy.

I was baffled. Hadn't she heard me—all of the disgusting things I did? I sniffled and looked back at my hands, "So, do you think I'm a terrible person?"

Melissa frowned. "Are you kidding me? You're a warrior, Cindy. None of this was your fault. You know that, don't you?"

I kept my gaze fixed on my hands and shrugged. *It wasn't my fault.* I had never heard those words before. Amid all the emotions weighing me down, the huge burden of guilt that I had been carrying for years suddenly seemed a touch lighter. Someone thought I wasn't to blame—and maybe I wasn't.

"Cindy, seriously. This wasn't your fault. Kip Arnold is a sick man. He's disgusting. You were a kid, and he was—he is—a predator. He preyed on you, and he tried to do the same thing to my sister. Honestly, who knows how many other girls he's tried this stuff on?"

I looked up at her. Hearing someone else echo what I had been wondering about Kip Arnold made the reality of the situation sink in.

Other girls.

The thought stole my breath. It wasn't just me. It was Marisol and me, for starters. Maybe others, too. *Probably* others. He was still teaching, and he had been a teacher at another school before he came to my school.

How. Many. Other. Girls.

In an instant, my world exploded. It wasn't just about me and my pain. Or just about me fighting for my family. Suddenly my vision was filled with all of the other women and girls he had ever come in contact with.

Other girls he had made uncomfortable. Other girls he had tried to groom. Other girls he had acted inappropriately with. Other girls he had assaulted and raped. How many other girls, how many other women were out there looking over their shoulders to make sure he wasn't following them—just like me? How many other girls were caught in the never-ending cycle of hating what Arnold did to them but feeling unable to officially cut ties with him? How many others were there, and if he was still teaching, how many more girls *would there be* if he wasn't stopped?

That thought stopped me in my tracks. It's one thing for fellow survivors to come together and support one another, and it certainly would make me feel less alone to spend time with the other women he targeted. But if he was still allowed to teach and be around kids, then he wasn't going to stop. Despite what he said to me, I knew he didn't love me. Of course, I knew I wasn't his soulmate, but I also knew *he* didn't think I was either. Plus, the final months of his involvement in my life had been so hostile; I'm sure he got tired of the constant fighting. I'm sure he was ready to find someone a bit easier to manipulate. What if he was looking for someone new to groom at that very moment?

The thought of some other little girl, who was just as naïve as I was at fourteen, coming in contact with him sent me into a panic. I wanted to scream. I wanted to jump in front of her and shield her from the awful man who had stolen my childhood and my innocence and left me so hopeless that I had contemplated suicide. If I wasn't his only victim, then he wasn't just a predator; he was a threat to every child in his proximity. And he was cunning, so he would carefully choose girls who would be just as afraid to speak up as I was. Maybe they would have parents who didn't come to their defense like Marisol's did; maybe their parents would be more like mine and either not notice or care about Arnold's involvement in their kid's life. As the abuse intensified, they'd fall deeper and deeper into the pit I was currently in. But what if I spoke up? If I shared what happened to me, could I maybe keep him from hurting anyone else?

But there was another, more personal, question I had to grapple with: would protecting a theoretical child from the potential long-term abuse I experienced be worth risking the man I loved and the family we were building? Honestly, I wasn't sure, but I knew one thing for certain: I had told someone my story and she didn't hate me. She didn't think I was a slut or that I was disgusting. She thought I was a *survivor*.

CHAPTER NINE
THE STAKEOUT

The more I thought about my conversation with Melissa about Marisol's interactions with Arnold, the more certain I became. This wasn't just about me and my own wellbeing anymore. If Arnold had also targeted Marisol, there were probably other girls too. And as long as he was still allowed to be around children, the list of people he tried to groom could be endless. I couldn't keep this secret in anymore, but what I was supposed to do? I was nearly twenty-two years old. It had been years since I had last spoken with Arnold, years since he last raped me. I was a legal adult and had a kid of my own. Would anyone even care if I came forward with what he did to me?

Sharing my story with Melissa felt like releasing a big breath that I had been holding in for years. I wondered if it would feel that same way with Juan, and if I let go of this dark secret between us, maybe I would feel even freer. Then if I found a way to speak out against Arnold, he wouldn't have any ammunition against me to scare me into silence. If Juan already knew, how could Arnold manipulate me into staying silent? I needed to tell Juan the truth—to use my voice, my words. Even if I wasn't able to do anything to stop Arnold, I knew speaking up would finally give me some peace and start the healing process.

Unfortunately, Juan wasn't as receptive to my story as Melissa when I first told him. While I didn't give Juan a grisly recap of everything Arnold did to me—I didn't think he'd be able to handle the stark facts—I hit on the main points: Kip Arnold groomed me and sexually assaulted me multiple times, all while we were together.

"Wait, you were sleeping with your old gym teacher? The whole time we were together?"

I was quiet for a moment, and then said, quietly, "I wasn't sleeping with him, Juan. It's not like we were dating or anything. He just got me in these situations and took advantage of me. And then he'd threaten me, so I was too scared to say anything." I could see in Juan's face that he was furious. Unlike when I spoke with Melissa, he wasn't just mad at Arnold; he was also mad at me.

"I just don't understand how you could let this happen for so long. If he really took advantage of you, why didn't you tell someone?"

Tears streamed down my face. "Juan, I told you he scared me. He took advantage. He threatened. I didn't know what else to do. I didn't want to lose you or make you think less of me. But I didn't know how to make it all stop."

Juan threw up his hands in frustration. "You say *stop*, Cindy! That's how! You tell the cops! You tell your parents! You tell me! Someone!"

"I could tell *my* parents? Juan, I was fourteen the first time anything happened! I didn't even understand what he did to me! And you know as well as I do that my parents wouldn't have done anything! My mom let me keep talking to him on the phone! She didn't care! I was alone!"

Juan shook his head. "That's not true. You had me. You could have told me."

I looked down at my hands and shook my head. "Juan, by the time you and I started dating, he'd already taken me to a hotel room. Things had already gotten out of control. I was broken when you met me."

"So you started dating me knowing that? Knowing you were going to still be with him?"

"I wanted to try to have a normal life. I thought I could get him out of my life on my own, but it just got worse."

Juan shook his head and rubbed the back of his neck in frustration. "So, is our baby even mine?"

I looked at Juan in disbelief. "Of course she's yours."

"Is she? Because apparently you weren't exactly faithful to me before she was born!"

Juan's words stung like a slap in the face. He saw Arnold's attacks as examples of times I was unfaithful. I wasn't a survivor in his eyes; I was a cheating girlfriend. And he reinforced the fears I'd had for years: If I truly didn't want the situation with Arnold, then I would have found a way to get Arnold out of my life for good long ago. Somewhere deep down, I must have wanted him to do those things to me. Somewhere deep down, maybe the times Arnold said things like, "Your mind's telling you no, but your body's telling you yes," he was right. Maybe I was disgusting trash like I had always feared. Because if Juan couldn't understand where I was coming from, who would?

"Juan, she's your child. But if you want to take a DNA test to prove it, I'm more than happy to do that. Because I'm certain she's yours. It was months after the last time he—"

"The last time you slept with him? Is that what you were going to say?"

I looked away, more tears escaping. "You were the only man I was sleeping with when she was conceived."

Juan shook his head as he paced around the room. "Why are you telling me this? If he's been out of your life for so long, why are you bringing this up now?"

"Because, Juan, this secret has been eating me up inside! It's been killing me! I don't want any more secrets, and I don't want to keep things from you. After talking with Melissa about everything, I think I might have to do something to stop him from doing this to anyone else."

"What do you mean?"

I shrugged. "He's still a teacher. He can still hurt other girls. He probably *has* hurt other girls. He might be hurting them right now. And I don't know if I can stop it, but I wanted to talk to you about it because I feel like if I can do something to help, I need to."

Juan leaned against the wall and rubbed his temples. "You're right. I hate it, but you're right. If he did this to you, and he could be doing this to others, then you need to say something. You should have said something a long time ago, but you need to say something now."

I nodded and looked at my hands as I absentmindedly picked at my fingers. I asked quietly, "Do you hate me? Are you going to leave?"

Juan closed his eyes. "I don't know, Cindy. This is a lot. You're telling me you were with this man for years while we were together, that you let him sleep with you, that you spent hours talking on the phone, and that you didn't tell anyone. I don't know if I can trust you. And now it's about to come out that my girlfriend, the mother of my child, was in this relationship for years? How do you think I feel about that?"

"It wasn't a relation—" I started, but then I stopped myself short and just nodded. I took a deep breath and started again. "I was young. I didn't know what to do, and I was trying to protect you."

Juan pushed himself off the wall and waved his arms in front of him. "I don't want to talk about this anymore. Let's talk to a lawyer about what your options are when it comes to reporting him, and we can go from there."

As I had feared, when I told Juan, he looked at me differently; he initially doubted me and thought less of me. Even though I was heartbroken over his harsh reaction, I still felt a bit lighter. Arnold no longer held power over me when it came to telling Juan the truth. I took that power back. I told Juan my story. I controlled the narrative, and I spoke my truth. I knew it would take time for Juan to process it all, but he wasn't packing up to leave me immediately, and I took that as a sign that he could eventually understand what I had really gone through. Plus, the fact that he thought Arnold did something bad enough to warrant a discussion with a lawyer or the police made me feel validated.

We found a good lawyer and met almost immediately to discuss what had happened to me. And I wanted this lawyer to know exactly what happened, so I spared no detail. While I had been vaguer with Juan and Melissa, I was as graphic as possible with the lawyer to ensure he had all the facts before he discussed our legal options.

I told my story for the third time then and it became a little easier with each retelling. The sting of the secret disappeared, and I felt emboldened. I still struggled to decide if I was a victim, a survivor, or if I had made choices that allowed (or welcomed) his abuse to continue in my life. But, at the same time, I began to fully accept that what he did to me was wrong, and I didn't want anyone else to experience it. I was done letting Arnold hold the power over me to keep me silent. I planned to tell people what he did, because if my words could save even one girl from a fate like mine, speaking out would be worth it.

After I shared everything with my lawyer, I looked at him anxiously. His brow was furrowed, and I could tell he was thinking carefully about his next words. Slowly, he leaned forward and looked at me.

"Thank you for telling me your story, Cindy. And I want you to hear me when I say what happened to you was wrong and it wasn't your fault."

I let out a sigh of relief. I desperately wanted that reaction from Juan, but it still felt great to hear someone tell me that I hadn't asked for any of Arnold's attacks. The lawyer and I continued to talk, and I ultimately decided it was best to file an official report with the police. I left the lawyer's office with some contact information, a plan, and a new boost of courage.

I went to the police immediately after my meeting with the lawyer and shared my story with two detectives. Once again, I held nothing back, and with every word I spoke, the sting of recounting the abuse was less painful. The weight of the horrible secret I kept lifted a little more. Although I felt some pressure talking to the detectives, unlike the time I was interrogated at my school, the entire room felt considerably less hostile. I could tell the detectives were listening intently to my story, checking to make sure there weren't any holes or inconsistencies. But they weren't looking at me like some kid who was trying to get away with something, and they weren't like the administration at the school, trying to cover themselves to avoid a scandal. I felt like they were actually on my side.

When I finished, one of the detectives spoke up almost immediately. "Cindy, I believe you. But there's a problem. It's been years since anything happened, and it's been even longer since he attacked you while you were a minor. We don't have any proof to get him on this one."

My heart sank. "So there's nothing we can do? I mean, he's still teaching. What if he does this to someone else?"

The detective nodded. "I know. That's why we've got to try something a little tricky if we want to pin this on him. But I've got to warn you, you might not like what I'm about to say."

Instinctively, I leaned back. "What are you thinking?"

"I want to set up a sting operation. If we can get evidence of him admitting to raping you when you were a minor, then we can take him in. But the thing is, if we're going to do this, you're going to have to reach out to him again."

Just the thought of contacting Arnold again sent my mind spinning. I remembered the last time I had reached out to him after a prolonged absence. It had ended in more heartache and new opportunities for him to rape me. I hated the idea of letting him back into my life, and I was terrified of doing anything that could potentially expose my daughter to Kip Arnold. What would he do if I suddenly resurfaced in his life? He claimed to be a vengeful person. If he found out I was part of a sting operation, would he track me down and attack me in the night? What if he tried to hurt Juan or my daughter? Would the police protect me? Would I have to uproot my life to keep my family safe from him?

The detective could see the fear in my eyes, and he held up his hands. "I know it's a tall order to reach out to him again. But I want you to think about it. We'd keep you safe, we'd be with you the entire time, and we'd be monitoring your calls. If we're able to do this right, we can get him thrown in jail where he couldn't hurt you or anyone else again."

After that, I talked it over with Juan. "If I did this sting operation, we might be able to send him to jail. But that would mean the story would get out. It'd be a big deal, and a lot of people we know might hear about this part of my life. And we could go through with the whole sting operation, and it might not work. If we can't get him to admit what he did, then we'll have nothing. Do you think it's worth it?"

Juan nodded. "I think you should do it. We can deal with whatever comes next, and this guy needs to go to jail. I don't want anyone else to deal with what you and I are dealing with right now."

After we discussed the idea in depth, I returned to the detectives to agree to the sting operation. The plan was a simple one. I'd call Arnold, talk with him on the phone a few times, and convince him I wanted to reconnect. We worked up a story that would explain my long absence. I had the baby, but Juan left me. So I was a single mother, struggling to make ends meet, and I needed Arnold. I'd tell him he was right and that Juan had treated me exactly as Arnold predicted. I knew it would be exactly what he wanted to hear, and it would reignite our conversations. From there, I'd try to get him to reminisce about old times to see if I could get him on record admitting to raping me when I was a minor.

I would be using a phone that the police officers would monitor, so I wouldn't have to deal with my phone buzzing constantly during the day. The police also assured me that if I was ever worried about seeing Arnold around, I could call them. The plan was in motion, and I was ready to get started.

Even though Juan supported me as I went to the authorities, our relationship was still tense. And it only got worse when his mother found out. Her reaction was similar to Juan's, questioning why I didn't say anything years ago. She didn't understand how anyone could let something get that far, and she was convinced that if I really wasn't happy with the physical things Arnold did to me, I would have done something.

On top of all of that, she didn't like the idea of the woman her son had a baby with holding on to such a dark secret and being "unfaithful" to her son. Her reaction colored Juan's own response, and it seemed that if I started to make some headway with him when it came to understanding the ways Arnold had groomed me and manipulated me, one conversation with his mother would undo all of our progress. Still, we weren't ready to give up on each other. And with the sting operation about to go down, we both knew our lives would become incredibly intense, and we'd have to support each other like never before.

The detectives knew I had destroyed my old phone, so they asked if I remembered Arnold's phone number. Of course I did. I had seen it on my phone nearly every day for years, and sometimes I even had dreams about fielding calls from him. I had lots of nightmares where I looked down, saw my old phone as I was sitting in Juan's house, and the screen started flashing with Arnold's number. So, remembering the number wasn't a problem.

But Arnold wasn't quick to answer the phone. He didn't recognize the number, so he didn't pick up right away. When he finally did and realized it was me, he acted like no time had passed. It was almost as if he expected me to call him. As if, for all these years, he had told himself that I'd ultimately come crawling back.

"How's your day been going, Cindy?"

"Uh," I stammered, shocked at his familiarity. "It's okay, I guess. How are you?"

"I'm fine. You have the baby?"

I shook my head to get my thoughts straight. "Uh, yeah, I did. It's a... it's a boy," I lied. "He's great."

"That's good to hear. How's Chunti?"

"Well, I'm not with him anymore."

"You don't say."

I sighed and tried to put as much strain into my voice as I could, "I know. It's just like you said. He left me. I've been on my own, trying to raise our kid. It's been so hard."

"I'm not gonna say I told you so, but—"

"You were right. You were right about all of it." I looked up at the detectives who were monitoring the calls. One of them gave me a thumbs up and mouthed for me to direct the conversation to the rapes. "You know, I've been so lonely and so depressed lately, it's got me thinking about old times."

"Oh yeah," Arnold said, an edge to his voice.

"Do you remember the first time you kissed me? That day in the storage room?"

"No."

I frowned. I knew he was lying. Panic stricken, I looked up at the detectives. They mouthed for me to try again. I sighed. "Stop playing. I know you remember! I was fourteen, you were the fancy new P.E. teacher on campus, and you told me to meet you in the storage closet."

"Why are you talking like this? Are you with the cops?"

I froze, and the detectives frantically started motioning for me to direct the conversation back to the task at hand. "The cops? What for? It's been so long, if I was going to talk to the cops, wouldn't I have done that already? I told you, I'm just sad and lonely. I need help. I need you. Being a single mom is hard, and you were always so good to talk to when I was having a hard day."

"We did have some good times, huh?"

I smiled. I could hear him lowering his guard, and I continued to press to get him to admit to the rapes. It took several phone calls, and though I knew it was for a good cause, it made my skin crawl to act so saccharine-sweet with him. But as I pushed him to reminisce about "old times," he eventually admitted to the rapes. He even started to revert to his old behaviors, ringing up the phone at all hours. He would call or text so frequently that the cops who were monitoring the phone would talk about how he was driving them all nuts.

However, something must have felt a bit off to Arnold. We were able to get him on record admitting to everything, but he started acting paranoid. Every time we talked, we went from "reminiscing" about old times and having a pleasant conversation to him turning on a dime to ask about the police. Suddenly, he yelled something like, "Oh my gosh, you're with the cops right now, aren't you? I can't believe I didn't see it before!"

After a few calls, I became a pro at responding to accusations like that. I knew I needed to stay calm so I could convince him to calm down and stay on the line. Without missing a beat, I always said something like, "Relax. I told you. It's been so long. If I was going to tell the police about you, I would have done it years ago. What's the point of doing that now?" With that, he would relax again, but it never took long before I said say something that made him flip right back into a state of panic.

I'm not sure what set him off, but he constantly flipped between unbridled terror over police involvement and sounding happy to talk with me. Maybe it was because I seemed so keen to talk about things that I'd always tried desperately to steer the conversation away from up to that point. Maybe I didn't sound as familiar or comfortable in our conversations as I thought I did. Whatever the reason, I spent a lot of time trying to stop him from obsessing over the police. And while he didn't stop the phone calls, according to the officers that were watching his house, he had stopped going home entirely. When we had our final phone call, he was certain I was setting him up.

"Cindy, I can't sleep anymore. I'm going crazy over here. I haven't been staying at my house because I just know the cops are after me. I've been running from my demons for so long, and they've finally caught up with me. I'd just rather die than go to jail. I'll kill myself before I let the cops take me in. I don't want my family to find out. I have a daughter, you know."

I frowned. He had casually mentioned a daughter a few times years ago, but he rarely talked about her. I never saw her, he didn't have pictures of her in his house, and I could probably count on one hand the times he brought her up prior to the sting operation. I knew what he was doing by mentioning his estranged daughter. He was trying to make me feel guilty and relent, but I wasn't falling for it this time. He wasn't about to guilt trip me into letting him off the hook for a daughter who clearly wasn't even a part of his life anymore.

I pressed on and tried to calm him down. The fear in his voice was palpable, and I began to worry that he'd get desperate enough to take his own life before the police reached him. I shot a panicked look at one of the officers near me as I laughed brightly and said, "What are you talking about?" The officer held up a hand to calm me down and encouraged me to diffuse the situation. "I've said it before, and I'll say it again. Why would you think I'm working with the police now?"

Arnold laughed bitterly. "Call it a gut instinct? I don't know. Just, please do me the kindness of telling me if that's what you're doing. I can't go to jail. I won't. I'm serious; I'll kill myself before that ever happens. I just—I don't feel right about any of this, and I'm going crazy with worry. Please. I need to go home. I need to sleep. Just tell me if you're working with the cops."

I did my best to convince him I wasn't tricking him, and the police seemed pretty convinced that he was lying about attempting suicide. However, they were sure he would try to escape, so they planned to go after him before he could skip town. Reassured that he would ultimately face justice, I couldn't help but smile at the sound of his panicked voice. For so many years, he had complete control of our interactions and over me. For so many years, he had manipulated my words, my needs, my fears, and my desires to get what he wanted. Now, for the first time ever, that power dynamic had been flipped, and he was losing it. I wasn't a kid he could control, and I wasn't some scared student trying to navigate high school, college, a relationship, and the abuse of a former substitute teacher. I was a mother. A fighter. I was powerful and that scared him—and I relished it.

Once we had Arnold on tape admitting to the abuse—and with the added pressure of Arnold's threats of suicide—the police didn't waste time organizing a way to take him into custody. I knew we had a long way to go, but I felt so vindicated. I hid for so many years, trying to rationalize away the abuse I was suffering. But now I stood there with no more secrets, bravely sharing my scars and letting people know that something bad had happened to me and I wasn't going to shove it under a rug anymore. I was taking back my power and using my voice. Through my actions, the man who had made my life a living hell was about to be arrested.

Arnold wasn't staying at his house, and he told me he was staying somewhere far away. It turned out that wasn't true, and he was actually staying in a place pretty close to his house. So it wasn't hard for officers to track him down at a nearby gas station. While I was busy driving with Juan to conduct a few interviews in another part of town, a couple of officers approached Arnold while he was gassing up his truck. Arnold immediately became defensive when he realized who they were.

"Look, I know why you're coming for me, and let me just tell you that I'm going to kill myself before I let you guys take me in," Arnold warned. Then he hopped in his truck and took off.

The police were right behind him. I got an urgent call from them, telling me that they were in a car chase with Kip Arnold and that I needed to report to the station immediately. I went to the station and sent Juan on to finish up a normal workday as I anxiously watched the news coverage of my longtime abuser's police chase live on television.

The footage made it clear that Arnold wasn't exaggerating when he told the police how desperate he was to stay out of jail. A common tactic police use when attempting to stop a high-speed pursuit is something called a pit maneuver. Essentially, a police car intentionally bumps into the vehicle they're chasing, causing a crash that hopefully stops the chase. Police did this to Kip Arnold twice that day. And at first, it seemed like they had him. One of the pit maneuvers even wedged the bed of his truck under the trailer of a semi, but whether it was desperation or luck, Arnold managed to get control of his truck and drive away from each attempt to stop him.

However, car chases rarely end well for the person evading police. It almost always ends with the person ditching their car, heading out on foot and ultimately getting caught, or getting tangled in a pit maneuver or a barricade and getting arrested. I think Arnold was beginning to realize that he wouldn't be able to evade the police forever. Still certain he'd rather die than go to jail, he drove his truck off the road, through a guard rail, and off a cliff. His car careened into the ground below and managed to slam into a nearby tree.

The officers erupted in shouts of shock and frustration when that happened. The chase was clearly over, but Arnold's fate was unclear. Had he died? Did he hurt someone? Was he escaping on foot? What was happening? All I could think as I watched the footage on pins and needles was, *this idiot better not be dead; he better not get the easy way out.* While I wanted Arnold to never be in a position where he could hurt kids again, I also wanted justice. For me. For Marisol. For any other girls he had hurt who hadn't come forward. I didn't want him just wiped off the planet in a ridiculous car chase. I wanted him to face the music, look me in the eye, know it was me who turned him in, and have to own up to the horrible things he did to me. I did not want him to wriggle out of accountability and consequences because he killed himself before due justice could be served.

It wasn't long before we realized he was pinned in his truck but alive. He had to be airlifted from the wreck, but paramedics were able to get to him and take him to a hospital. We found out later that he was injured, but he would make it. He was in custody, and he would have to own up to everything he did to me in the form of seven felony charges, such as lewd acts on a child, oral copulation on a child under sixteen, and sexual penetration by a foreign object. And to top it all off, he had one felony charge of evading the police.

Juan and I were still working through our issues, and we had good days and bad. I started attending therapy to work through my trauma. But as I did that, and Juan and I worked through our trust issues together, it was so healing for both of us to know that Arnold was finally being held accountable. The courts affirmed that what he did to me was wrong and worthy of multiple felony charges.

I didn't sit in the courtroom for most of the proceedings, though I did share a statement at the end of the trial. I was able to come face to face with Arnold, and for the first time ever, I was able to speak my truth to him, express my feelings and needs—and he just had to sit in silence and listen. I didn't have to deal with him undermining, manipulating, or gaslighting me. Finally, he didn't have an ounce of power to influence my words.

Through the court proceedings, it came to light that he had actually been dismissed on a sexual harassment charge brought up by the aide working for him where he taught before he started subbing at my school. However, the accusations hadn't stuck, and there was no formal charge. Not that it mattered. My school district hadn't thought it important to do a thorough background check during Arnold's hiring process—that dismissal would have absolutely come up had they done their due diligence.

In essence, my school district had thrown open its doors and let a predator come prowling inside.

Because of that, I was even more motivated to do whatever I could to get him thrown in jail for a long time. This one would stick. He would be a registered sex offender. He would spend the rest of his life in jail. He would never be allowed near kids again. I was done feeling afraid of him. I was boldly telling my story, sharing how I survived years of his abuse—and I wasn't afraid to rock the boat. I had a voice, and I needed to be heard. It was Kip Arnold's turn to be afraid of me.

And boy, I wish I could tell you that's exactly what happened. But in reality, he managed to get a plea bargain. Some of the felony charges did stick, and he is officially a registered sex offender, but he was released from prison in two and a half years—less time than he spent abusing me.

CHAPTER TEN
SEVERING TIES

We love to hear that bad guys "get theirs" in the end. Learning that Kip Arnold would serve less than three years for stealing so much from me felt outrageously unfair. I started to wonder if it had all been worth it. Had I risked my mental health, my safety, my family's safety, and my reputation all for nothing? At first, I think I couldn't help but feel that maybe his paltry sentence had ultimately trivialized all those years of pain. Yes, I was proud of myself for speaking up and standing my ground, but to go through everything I did—summon the courage to make myself vulnerable by sharing my story with lawyers, friends, Juan, police officers, and the entire court—only for him to run off with such a light sentence? Where was the justice in that?

It was at that point I understood something important: I didn't speak up for Kip Arnold. I didn't survive the hell he'd put me through for *him*. In my decision to seek justice, I was severing ties with Kip Arnold for good. I was officially kicking him out of my life and starting to write my own story, in my own words—not a version of events dictated by my abuser. And I wasn't about to start that new life by trading the huge burden of shame and fear for a burden of disappointment and frustration because the court system didn't do its job like I'd hoped.

Even though I wanted justice, I was able to separate Arnold's legal consequences from my journey of healing. I realized his sentence didn't have any impact on the power I was able to reclaim in my life, and it didn't have any bearing on me finally finding my voice. And my newfound sense of hope and healing continued to grow every time someone said to me, "Kip Arnold wronged you, and he was at fault, not you." Of course, I still had people in my life like Juan, Juan's mother, and my own mother who were not as quick to assign blame solely to Kip Arnold. But finding the courage to use my voice in such a powerful, scary way and having so many people affirm my words and choices gave me a new lease on life. All of the work Arnold and my parents had done over the years to silence me and break down my confidence and strength was slowly but surely being undone.

Better yet, I realized I was able to stop this from happening to anyone else—at least at the hands of Kip Arnold. Arnold had gained access into my life through school and the negligence of my school district. If he had never been a substitute for my class, I would have had no other reason to meet him and none of this would have happened. However, because of the way my school district failed to conduct a proper background check, he was able to walk through the door unhindered. If Mr. Valdemar hadn't left it up to me to decode what he meant by "Sunshine, I don't like you spending so much time with Mr. Arnold" and had he spoken in frank terms—or, even better, filed a report with my school's administration or not allowed me to leave his class for Arnold's—then Arnold wouldn't have been able to escalate his behavior or get me alone on school property. So many members of my school's teaching staff and administration, along with the whole school district, failed me by not taking the responsibility of their roles seriously. And they continued to fail the rest of the students in my district when they reassigned Arnold rather than firing him after hearing about him driving me to my flag competitions.

I was on my own back then. My school and school district didn't care. My teachers didn't care. My parents didn't care. My sister didn't care. I had to use my sheltered, naïve, fourteen-year-old brain to try to navigate the very grown-up, very confusing world of manipulation, boundaries, and what to do when an adult crosses a line with a child. I wasn't equipped for that—no kid is. And because it was left to me to navigate all of that on my own, I got swept away, nearly for good. But once I found the courage to speak up, to call for help, and to finally tell someone what happened, Arnold would never get the chance to do that to another kid. Yeah, his prison sentence was short. But he'll be a registered sex offender for the rest of his life. Being a registered sex offender will come up every time he applies for a job. It will dictate where he can and cannot live.

The choices he made when he decided to harass the aide at his old school, abuse me for years, attempt to groom Marisol to be another of his victims, and any other abuse, rape, or harassment he potentially inflicted on other women or girls will haunt him forever. I got to be the ally for the other kids Arnold might have encountered and the protector that I wish I had all those years ago. When I agreed to participate in that sting operation, I stood up for myself and reclaimed my story—and that personal victory didn't hinge on the years Arnold spent in jail.

Was I frustrated and upset to hear Arnold didn't spend the rest of his life in jail? Of course. Is it hard to process and accept that as I'm writing this, as far as I know, Kip Arnold is out of jail and living as a free man? Absolutely. But I was and still am done with letting him dictate my moods and my future. I broke the connection with him for good, and I took back my story to heal myself and protect others. And that feels like a huge win to me.

However, trauma is a complicated thing to beat. Despite the personal victory I felt after Arnold's criminal proceedings ended and my newfound strength, I was still nursing a mortal wound in the pit of my soul—one I ignored for years. My relationship with my parents was as strained as ever, and though my dad still doesn't seem to know much about the case, my mother does. She was mortified and ashamed when she found out—and she let me know. Her words were painful and hard to hear, especially because they came while I was still in a cycle of trying to heal my relationship with Juan. We would work to reconcile as I tried to help him understand what happened, and then backtrack when his mom would say something cruel or careless about my responsibility in stopping Arnold. On top of all of that, I was riddled with fear, shame, confusion—not to mention, I had developed terrible coping mechanisms to deal with my trauma after years of trying to hide such a dark secret.

Ultimately, therapy was not only key in helping me heal, but it was also instrumental in helping me change the way I thought about what happened to me. I used to think therapy was mainly about looking forward, accepting my current circumstances so I could move on with life in a happy and healthy manner. And it definitely does serve that purpose, but I quickly realized that if I wanted to heal myself where I stood in that moment, I needed to go back and heal wounds from the past. I would have to relive what had happened and process those experiences with new eyes and the support of my therapist; only then could I find the healing to move on with my life.

People love to use the cliché about treating a bullet wound with a band-aid, and for so long that was the method I tried to use. Arnold's involvement in my life, the tension in my home life, and the years of burying the secret of it deep in my heart had pierced my spirit with a big bullet hole. And I was trying to slap a band-aid on it to move on. The last thing

I wanted to do was relive what had happened to me, and the thought of processing the rapes and the trauma felt incredibly scary and exhausting. But once I started working through the trauma with my therapist, I was amazed at how healing it was. Every time we talked about my experience, it hurt less. Every time we processed through my feelings, I was able to let go of another layer of guilt and shame.

For one thing, I didn't realize how much blame I heaped on myself or how much responsibility I placed on my fourteen-year-old shoulders for what Arnold—a full-grown adult—did to me. It was a completely foreign idea to me that I, through my actions, hadn't somehow welcomed his advances and "asked for" any of his attacks. I was certain that if I had spoken to him differently, dressed differently, or reacted to his actions in some other way, then he wouldn't have abused me.

But my therapist helped me realize that Arnold targeted me because I was a child who didn't know any better. He targeted me because he knew I didn't have the support system at home to protect me or let me know when his behavior had crossed a line. He targeted me because he realized I had the perfect set of experiences and circumstances to have someone swoop in, groom me, manipulate me, and warp my mind so I wouldn't see his involvement in my life as predatory. I came to understand that, yes, I could have reacted differently to the things he did to me but the blame wasn't mine to carry. The blame rested solely on the shoulders of the adult who absolutely abused his position of authority.

I came to that realization, released some of that blame, and began to see my former self not as a stupid, selfish, disgusting person, but as a child who was alone, confused, and scared; a little girl trapped in a situation she never should have been in to begin with. Grasping this didn't just change me, though. As I started to heal and truly know I wasn't at fault for what happened, I began to speak more openly to Juan about what happened. I slowly began revealing parts of the story that I had kept from him, either due to shame or a desire to not upset him. And the more I talked to him about what I survived, the more I was able to explain how Arnold had kept me quiet for so long. I was able to explain about grooming and gaslighting, and how the lack of concern from both my parents and my school perpetuated the belief that I was mistaken for feeling uncomfortable with Arnold's actions.

It took years. It took therapy. It took patience—from me and Juan. It took love. It took respect. And most surprisingly, it took a healthy dose of Jesus. But ultimately, I was able to get to a place where I felt strong again, and Juan and I were finally able to come together. Juan was able to hear my heart and understand that I had survived something horrific and realized that he was wrong to heap the blame on me. Our relationship became stronger than ever, and the work we did to reconcile, understand, and heal together led to a family that I can't imagine living without. We got married, we've had two more beautiful babies, and our business is thriving. I can say without a shadow of a doubt, my future is so bright. I can't wait to see what comes next for me and for us.

That's not to say my trauma is gone. Trauma, especially intense, prolonged trauma like the stuff I went through, leaves scars. And sometimes it flares back up in ways I don't expect. I'm still hypervigilant in public. I always take notice of the men around me; there are still smells, men with a similar build to Arnold, and mannerisms that either send warning signals to my brain or send me into a state of panic. To this day, there are still times when I struggle with being intimate with Juan, and there are still parts of my story that I'm only just beginning to feel comfortable sharing with him.

The difference is that those feelings don't destroy me anymore, and I don't deal with them alone in the dark. If I start to feel frantic or worried in public, Juan knows what I'm thinking about, and he knows how to help me calm down. If we are getting intimate and I start to freeze up, he knows to stop and talk me through my feelings. He makes sure I never feel abandoned or alone, and he's always there to support me.

Faith has also played a huge role in us coming together and my healing. Though we both were raised in families that had a cultural involvement in their faith, it wasn't ever personally important to either one of us; I also actively pushed against Christianity in my teenage years. But toward the end of 2019, I became curious about Jesus. I had continued my therapy, but I still felt unable to fully move forward. My relationship with Juan was a bit rocky at the time too because of the stress of our work and my trauma triggers. I felt full of bitterness and anger that I still couldn't let things go after all of these years. I realized I was missing something in my life, and I needed to find something to give me lasting peace. So I began to search. I explored meditation a bit, but that only gave me some temporary peace. Then, one day, we ran into a friend who was a pastor, and he asked to pray for us. I was so overwhelmed with a feeling of peace and safety during the prayer that I had to know more.

I wanted to learn more about Jesus and understand what a relationship with Him was all about. And the more I learned about Jesus, His love for His people, and the way He works in our lives, the more I knew I needed Christ in my life. I accepted Him into my heart, was baptized, and suddenly felt that I had a brand-new outlook on my past and my future. Finding Jesus and having a physical example of dying to my old life and being reborn in Christ through my baptism was such a powerful moment for me.

For the first time in my life, I felt Jesus take the weight of all of the shame, the guilt, and the pain of my past off my shoulders as I laid everything at His feet. He made a home in my heart in my broken state and made me new. I was restored, I was loved, and I was free. Therapy was helping me let go of the blame I felt, but my relationship with Jesus helped me see how much profound and inherent worth I had and will always have in His eyes. I wasn't disgusting or stupid to Him. I was before His eyes on the cross, and because of that, He loved me unconditionally.

For so long, I kept my pain hidden in a dark corner, nearly buckling under the weight of the burdens of secrets and shame that I carried. I was so afraid to speak out, mainly because of the shame I'd feel when the horrible things Arnold did to me came to light. But the thing is, Jesus is light. He brings light to the darkness, and while that might seem terrifying when you're stuck in the middle of a dark place, experiencing His grace, love, and the light He brings is freeing. He brought His light into the darkest, most upsetting, bleakest corners of my life. His truth exposed the secrets I clung to most tightly, and in the face of all of that, He still loved me. I was so priceless to Him, and He still wanted a relationship with me. I wasn't too damaged, too broken, too disgusting, too shameful, too anything for Jesus. His love made me feel so safe that, even when I gave Him my darkest secrets, I didn't feel fear or shame—only grace and love.

Even more amazing, the healing I experienced through therapy and growing closer to Jesus showed me the ways He had worked in my life, even in the darkest moments. He had placed Juan in my life, knowing that he would ultimately become the man I needed to support me as I walked away from Arnold for good. He put Juan's parents in my life to give us a safe place to land when I needed to move out of my parents' house and to teach me how to be a part of a family. He put Melissa and Marisol in my life to tell me that I wasn't alone and motivate me to speak up. And He gave me my beautiful daughter to help light the fire of strength and determination within me that for years had been so brutally snuffed out.

I realized that though I didn't understand why I had to walk the path I did, Jesus had been there the entire time. Without Him, I would either be dead or still ensnared in Arnold's awful web. The darkness of this fallen world had tried to swallow me up, but Jesus never gave up on me. He saw my potential and my worth. He had so much love for me and wasn't about to leave me alone. Once I welcomed Him into my heart, He started healing my wounds and making me whole. Right then, I got to experience such amazing freedom from the pain, fear, and shame that had held me captive. Juan experienced something just as powerful in his own encounters with Jesus and accepted Jesus into his heart as well.

Discovering our own relationships with Jesus gave us a rock on which we were able to build our lives and rebuild our relationship. I have no doubt that understanding Jesus' grace and love toward us helped Juan look at me and the parts of my story that he struggled to understand with more grace and love. It certainly helped me look at the darker parts of my own past that way. And the idea of receiving new life in Christ and being made whole was such a beautiful and life-changing thing for someone who once thought they were too broken to be fixed and too lost to be saved.

As you might expect, Juan and I both are incredibly vigilant with our children and do what we can to be sure our kids are safe at school without becoming the overly involved and annoying helicopter parents. We have spent a lot of time talking with our kids' school to ensure we know where they find their teachers, the process that a new teacher goes through from interview to their hire date, and the procedures that are in place should a teacher cross a boundary. We also work hard to make our children feel loved and supported, and as a rule, we don't keep big secrets from one another. Should something awful happen, we've worked to help our kids feel safe coming to us, knowing we'll never judge them and that we'll always love them.

As I look at myself now, I no longer see my instincts, my reactions, my thoughts, and my concerns as things that are misinformed or wrong. I understand that a lot of those instincts and reactions were built on ever-increasing trauma that started with my parents and ballooned to new heights when Arnold entered the picture. They were coping mechanisms that my body developed to help me survive. Thanks to the freedom, restoration, and hope I have in Jesus; the love and support of my husband; therapy; and for the sake of my children, I am able to see those reactions for what they are. I'm able to look at my younger self and say, "Hey, we don't have to worry anymore. We're safe. We don't have to hide." I'm able to appreciate those things my younger self did to survive—the secrets, being careful to not rock the boat, and keeping my pain inside at all times—but I'm also able to get her out of the driver's seat of my life. And now understanding the role Jesus has had in my life, I'm able to see that I was never truly alone, even when I was trying to understand very adult situations as a scared and lonely child. I'm here today because of Jesus, and I have the strength I have today because of Him. My children have a mom who is loving, silly, caring, fun, supportive, and involved in their lives because Jesus put the people in my life I needed to get out, get help, and rebuild my own life.

And on days when I feel overwhelmed or the pain of my past rears its ugly head, I'm also able to remember that by telling my story, I stopped Kip

Arnold from being able to get a job where he can hurt a child again. We were even able to take the school district to court over what they allowed to happen, and our actions forced the district as a whole to be accountable for how they hired new teachers and the policies they had in place to protect their students. So, when I think about myself at fourteen—the version of myself who is scared, confused, and alone—and I know that I've been able to protect another child from his influence, I am certain it was all worth it.

The traumatized version of myself isn't in the driver's seat anymore, and Kip Arnold doesn't have any place in my life either. I might have scars, but I'm strong. I might have trauma, but I have peace. I might have been alone for so long, but I've finally found faith, community, love, support, and family. And I might have been silent, but I've found my voice. I'm not afraid to show my scars anymore; they're part of what made me the woman I am today. As part of a community of survivors, I also know that when we all speak up, when we bravely show the world our scars and bring our secrets into the light, then those who inflicted those scars—the abusers, the predators, the gaslighters, and the manipulators—all lose a little bit of their power, and we are able to support one another and make the world a little bit safer.

I didn't really know how I wanted to start this book, but I certainly know how I want to finish it: If you're a survivor of abuse, I want you to know that there is hope. I found my voice, and I took back my life. I'm not defined by my past, but I'm not scared of it anymore, either. All of the horrible stuff I went through made me who I am and led me on the journey to find Juan and build our amazing family. I'm living a life full of joy and love with my husband and children, we have a thriving business, and I can honestly say that I am truly happy. I'm living a life I never dreamed I could have, and I wouldn't trade it for anything. I want you to know you can have that too. You're not too broken, you're not too lost, and you're not worthless. You're a warrior. You're a survivor. Your voice and your story are worth reclaiming, and I hope my story has given you the strength to tell yours.

EPILOGUE

If you're a survivor of abuse, here's the one message I want you to hear as you close this book: *What happened to you isn't your fault.* Like me, you might have people in your life who are telling you otherwise. But I want you to hear me when I say you didn't ask for it, you didn't make a choice, wear an outfit, drink a drink, or make a comment that made someone rape you. What happened to you was wrong, and you are so strong for surviving it.

I also encourage you to speak out if you can. Obviously, making sure you're safe is the first step, but if you're in a place where you can speak to a family member, friend, teacher, or the police, then do so. You deserve justice for what happened to you. But when survivors speak out, it can also protect that predator's future victims and sends a message to other predators that they will be held accountable.

For too long, victims of sexual assault, rape, and harassment have been silenced by shame, the stigma of sexual assault, and the misconception that the victim should have somehow prevented their attack. Female victims are so often called sluts, or told they were "asking for it." Male victims are often discarded entirely when they come forward, because people think "men can't be raped" or "a guy would never turn down sex." By perpetuating these stereotypes, we're adding to the survivors' trauma and—just like in my own experience—making survivors feel like they can't tell their story, get help, or find their way out of an abusive situation.

Despite what you might hear from others, what your attacker might say, and what you might fear is true, you aren't alone. There are so many other survivors out there waiting to support you and so many allies who are ready to stand with you. Your life is worth saving, and your voice isn't just worth hearing—the world *needs* to hear it. Abusers thrive when we keep their secrets. It's why they tend to spend so long manipulating and gaslighting us. We come to the point where we feel either too overwhelmed with shame to come forward or certain no one would believe us or care. Hearing Marisol's story gave me the courage to speak up and work with the police to get Arnold thrown in prison. And beyond that, Melissa offered me a helping hand when I needed it most, giving me encouragement, perspective, and telling me that what happened wasn't my fault. Hearing that changed everything for me. That's the power of our voices.

It also shows the power of support and community. Fear, shame, and misplaced blame kept me silent for so long. It is something that has driven a permanent wedge between me and my mother, it's a continuous point of contention between me and my mother-in-law, and it nearly destroyed my marriage. And it was through the apathy of my school district and my teachers that Arnold was able to find a place in my life at all. So, if you know a survivor, or if someone you love comes to you and says they're being abused—whether it's your friend, a family member, your child, or your partner—don't jump to a place of blame. Listen. Show empathy. Let that person know you're there for them and reassure them that it wasn't their fault. Don't be another reason for them to keep quiet. And if you're a teacher, administrator, or any other person in a position dealing with kids, take that responsibility seriously. Don't leave it up to the child to come to you and don't leave it up to the child to translate your vague warnings.

Protect children, protect one another, and don't create an environment for predators to lurk.

It's time we all found our voice. If you're a survivor, I hope you feel encouraged and empowered to speak your truth. And if you're a loved one of a survivor, I hope you feel encouraged to stand with and support them and to shut down those who seek to shame or silence us. It's time to rock the boat, friends. It's time to get loud. It's time to bring our secrets out of the shadows. So, let's find our voice, and let's stand up and speak out together. Let's make those who seek to hurt, abuse, and lurk in the shadows as predators feel scared of us. Let's take our power back, together.

ADDITIONAL RESOURCES

Need to talk to someone about what you've gone through? While you should always call 911 if you are in immediate danger, here are some places that are ready to extend a hand and help you out of that pit:

RAINN (Rape, Abuse, and Incest National Network). RAINN is one of the most extensive organizations for survivors of sexual assault. Though they specialize in supporting American survivors, they help people all over the world. You can visit rainn.org for a 24/7 live chat or call 800.656.4673. Their website also has a great deal of information about seeking help, reporting assault, and other helps, such as:

- Places to donate or volunteer to help survivors
- Resources to assist you in finding help in your area at centers.rainn.org
- Information about what to expect if you want to report your assault at rainn.org/reporting-and-criminal-justice-system
- Details on what to expect during a sexual assault forensic exam at rainn.org/articles/rape-kit
- Information about the sexual assault laws in your state at apps.rainn.org/policy

Me Too Movement. #MeToo trended nationwide to give people a safe place to disclose abuse, harassment, and sexual assault. Their website, metoomvmt.org/how-can-we-help-you gives you a place to seek help if you're actively in crisis, exploring healing, want to get help for a loved one, or want to join the movement. The website also features a safety exit to quickly divert you to a Google search page if you're investigating help in a place where it's not 100 percent safe.

Safe Helpline. If you are in the Department of Defense (DOD) community, visit safehelpline.org for resources. You can also explore safehelpline.org/live-chat if you need to talk with someone.

National Sexual Violence Resource Center. Visit nsvrc.org for resources for survivors, friends, family, advocates, and educators, as well as ways to volunteer and much more.

Male Survivor. For male survivors of sexual assault, malesurvivor.org offers resources for finding help, forums and chats to get help and support, and other forms of assistance.

1in6. For male survivors, 1in6.org also provides online chat support and resources. You can check out their chat options at 1in6.org/helpline.

Human Trafficking. If you or someone you love is being trafficked, you can reach out to the National Human Trafficking Hotline. Their website, humantraffickinghotline.org, has a lot of great information and statistics on trafficking, ways to stay safe, and resources. To get help, you can reach them on their website via a live chat, text 233733, or call 1.888.373.7888.

National Suicide Prevention Lifeline. If you are struggling with suicidal thoughts or suicidal ideation, you can head to suicidepreventionlifeline.org for a 24/7 live chat. You can also call 1.800.273.8255. The website has a vast array of resources concerning ways to get involved, resources if you have a loved one who is suicidal, resources to help you if you're feeling suicidal, and much more.

HELPFUL BIBLE VERSES

Going to the authorities was so important for my healing and bringing my secrets out of the shadows, but my faith also played a huge role in allowing me to feel freedom from the shame and fear Arnold heaped on me for so many years. If you are looking for some hope or encouragement, here are a few verses that have given me so much hope, peace, and perspective. I hope they will help you on your journey as well. I divided these verses into subject matter so you can more easily find the verses that speak to you where you are right now. Obviously, you can use whatever Bible translation you like, but if you're unsure where to start, I've always found the New International Version (NIV) to be the easiest to understand.

HEALING
Isaiah 53:5
Psalm 147:3
Jeremiah 17:14; 33:6
James 5:16

FREEDOM
Psalms 34:19; 118:5; 119:45
Isaiah 61:1
John 8:31-32,36
Romans 6:18; 8:1-2
2 Corinthians 3:17

Galatians 5:1
1 Peter 2:16

FORGIVENESS

2 Chronicles 7:14
Psalms 32:5
Joel 2:13
Matthew 6:12,14; 18:21-22
Luke 6:27,37
Ephesians 2:8-9
1 John 1:9

LOVE

John 3:16; 14:15
1 John 4:8,18

PEACE

Numbers 6:24-26
Psalm 4:8; 29:11
Isaiah 26:3; 54:10
John 14:27; 16:33
Romans 8:6
Philippians 4:6-7
2 Thessalonians 3:16

RESTORATION

Joel 2:25-26
Jeremiah 29:11

Mark 11:24
1 John 5:4

NEW LIFE

Jeremiah 1:5
Isaiah 64:8
Psalm 139:13-16
Matthew 6:33
Romans 9:20
Acts 2:38-39
2 Corinthians 5:17
Ephesians 2:10
1 Peter 1:23; 3:18-22

GLORY TO GOD

Psalm 72:19
John 17:4-5
Romans 3:23
1 Corinthians 10:31
2 Corinthians 10:17; 12:5-6
Galatians 6:14
Ephesians 2:8
Philippians 2:9-11; 4:11,13
James 1:17
1 John 4:4

ACKNOWLEDGMENTS

First and foremost, I want to give all of the glory to my Savior, Jesus Christ. Without Him, I wouldn't have a story to tell, so I want to thank Him for saving me, restoring me, making me whole, and giving me the courage to speak up and share my story in a way to help and save others. Second, I'd like to thank my husband, Juan, for being my backbone and my rock. Thank you for being with me through everything, showing me so much love and support through the years, and extending so much patience and grace toward me. You've been there for me in my best and worst moments, but through the good and the bad, you're always right by my side and I know I can always count on you to be there for me. Next, I'd like to thank Thomas Johnston for believing my story. You were the first person I told, and the first person who heard, in major detail, what happened to me. Thank you for making me feel heard, safe, and supported in that moment and empowering me to pursue justice through the courts. Thank you for being my advocate and ally throughout the whole process of the court case and believing me when I was certain no one ever would. Finally, thank you to Esther Fedorkevich, Danielle Hale, Tori Thacher, Deryn Pieterse, Stephanie Cross, Kendall Davis, and the entire team at The Fedd Agency for coming alongside me, believing in my story, and bringing it to life in this beautiful book.